"Anne Johnson has crafted meditations as timeless and ~~
seashells, that invite us to dive wh~'
of daily life and to
A beautiful and co~
—*Dr. Kathlyn*
Co-*author of* Conscious Loving  ... ~eart

"Sometimes we are given reminders in our lives that what looks and feels
like an obstacle is really a gift. When we do have such a realization, it
could be called grace in action. To watch another go through this process
of awakening can be a powerful blessing. *Return to the Sea* is one such
blessing. Here, we journey with Anne Johnson as she unravels some of
the mysteries of life's obstacles to transform them into beacons of light
on the path we all walk, in one way or another. How much easier it
would be to uncover the sometimes hidden treasures our lives hold if we
could remember to embrace the message in this book!"
—*Ann Ruethling, Chinaberry Book Service*

"Anne Johnson has found the key lesson in Anne Morrow Lindbergh's
Gift from the Sea. At times, we all need to return
to our private 'beach' to renew ourselves."
—*Dorothy Schaeffer, Assistant Airport Director (Retired)*
Minneapolis-St. Paul International Airport; Board Member of the Minnesota
Aviation Hall of Fame; Associate Member of the Lindbergh Foundation

"A simple and dignified recipe for the collection
of the seashells of the soul."
—*Jacquelyn Mitchard, Author of* The Deep End of the Ocean

Return to the Sea

Reflections on Anne Morrow Lindbergh's
GIFT FROM THE SEA

ANNE M. JOHNSON
FOREWORD BY REEVE LINDBERGH

Innisfree
Press, Inc.

A call to the
deep heart's core.

Published by Innisfree Press, Inc.
136 Roumfort Road
Philadelphia, PA 19119-1632

Cover image "Hatteras Whelk"
© 1985 by Sara Steele. All Rights Reserved.
Collection of Christina Sickles Merchant.

Cover and chapter title page design by Hugh Duffy.

Library of Congress Cataloging-in-Publication Data
Johnson, Anne M., date.
Return to the sea : reflections on Anne Morrow Lindbergh's
Gift from the sea / Anne M. Johnson ;
foreword by Reeve Lindbergh.
p.   cm.
ISBN 1-880913-24-0
1. Lindbergh, Anne Morrow, 1906– Gift from the sea.
2. Life.   I. Title
BD435.L523J64   1998   98-7368
170'82–dc21   CIP

in deepest gratitude
to
Anne Morrow Lindbergh

Anne Morrow Lindbergh
is known for many things:
her flying career with her husband, Charles Lindbergh,
the tragic kidnapping of their first child,
her writing of books for over forty years.
But perhaps she is most loved for the gift she gave
to millions of women in her thoughtful, meditative classic,
GIFT FROM THE SEA.

Contents

Foreword

I first read Anne Johnson's *Return to the Sea* while I was staying on Sanibel Island, in Florida, only a few miles from the beach on Captiva where my mother lived during the time she was writing *Gift from the Sea*, more than forty years ago. It was an odd feeling, to be reading this new book and thinking about the older one, looking out at that beach, walking along the same stretch of sand and picking up some of the very same shells that both my mother, Anne Morrow Lindbergh, and the writer, Anne Johnson, had contemplated as they wrote down their thoughts about their own lives, with words that reach out to touch the lives of women everywhere.

I found, and felt, a kind of double "returning," as I read *Return to the Sea*. First of all, I could identify closely with my mother's time on this beautiful coast, and I could feel within myself the rhythm she herself had felt, a kind of spiritual inhalation that accompanied every wave rolling in from the Gulf of Mexico. I could breathe in, with the warm salt-scented air, the philosophy that revealed itself to Anne Morrow Lindbergh throughout her long stretch of solitude, in the midst of the peace that marked those days. This was my first "returning," to my mother's life and thought.

Interestingly, though, there was a second returning, and a very different one. I found that as I was reading, and walking on this beach, I could identify just as closely, and perhaps even more closely, with the writing of a woman of my own time. Anne Johnson is a woman not too far from my own age, raising her children and pursuing her career in the 1990's, as I am doing. She is a writer, a reader, a wife and mother, a woman with a sustaining circle of friends. She could be me, or she could be you, and she knows the nature of our lives, right here and now, as my mother knew the lives of our mothers. The language of our generations is a little different, as it must be. The times are different, too.

"I want a singleness of eye," wrote my mother, Anne Lindbergh, "a purity of intention, a central core to my life." I have always taken her words to heart, have always been inspired by them, and touched deeply by her unique and eloquent writing voice, in *Gift from the Sea*. Today, though, I read in Anne Johnson's reflections on my mother's book another set of words, and they touch me, too.

"Now, if while I'm putting my daughter to bed, I catch myself reciting a litany of chores I have to do in my head, I slow my breath down, let go of the company of my thoughts, and feel present to the moment. When I remember to do this, my experience is transformed."

Suddenly, my own experience is transformed. I am bending over my own child, as I tuck him in at night, after a long day for both of us. I don't have a "singleness of eye" or a "purity of intention," but I have my mother's words in mind. Now, I have Anne Johnson's, too. I can "let go of the company of my thoughts, and feel present to the moment." All at once, the generations are joined, and the lives of women everywhere, from every time, come together.

Separated from one another by four decades, the books of these two Annes nonetheless resonate beautifully. I know the first one, *Gift from the Sea*, almost by heart, because it is written in my mother's voice, a voice I have loved above all others for so many years. But I think I will come to know the second, Anne Johnson's *Return to the Sea*, almost as well. I read it on a beach my mother knew during another time, and it has returned me to my mother, and to myself.

— *Reeve Lindbergh*

Introduction

As the deadline for completion of this book drew nearer, I found myself needing to get away. I had always managed to do my writing in between taking kids to school and picking them up again. In between answering the phone and letting the dog out. In between unloading the dishwasher, making beds, and sweeping the kitchen floor. But with less then a month remaining until my deadline, I knew I needed long hours of being alone to get clear about what I wanted to share in this book. I needed to do what Anne Morrow Lindbergh had said all along was necessary: Create time and space to be alone.

A day of phone calls and arrangements later, and I have done it: I am alone. At a Benedictine monastery. I have a bed and a bath. A chapel to pray in. A library to study in. Woods to walk in. The words above the fireplace in the lounge read . . . "That All May Be One."

I begin by thanking St. Benedict for his vision: a

lifestyle that includes time for solitude. I wonder if he had any idea, so many hundreds of years ago, that his monastic order would all but die out, that the rooms in buildings named after him would be inhabited by women—one being the likes of me, a mother of three in her late thirties, equipped with a computer and all the creature comforts I need to feel at home: pictures of my husband and children, the pillow and blanket from my own bed, my terry cloth robe. Even if he didn't, I thank him.

I walk, I eat, I nap. I get up and face my fears. Can I write this book? Can I share what is in my heart?

As I climb the stairs back to my room after my morning walk, I notice: There are only older women here. And only a few. Except for the woman who is employed as the center coordinator, and a girl I see watering the plants, the only women inhabiting this place, in search of solitude, are well beyond my age . . . white-haired and spry, but certainly beyond the years of having children at home or a busy and demanding career.

The place is all but empty. A beautifully renovated monastery nestled in quiet woods, overlooking a lake, ten minutes from a major university town. One night's lodging, including breakfast, costs less than a night at the movies with my family. I'd bet that within a radius of fifteen miles, hundreds of women thought or said in the last month, *I wish I could just get away by myself.* And this place is nearly deserted.

Has anything changed in the half century since Anne Morrow Lindbergh wrote *Gift from the Sea*? Will we women ever learn to love and honor ourselves enough to get away on a regular basis to feed our souls? How many of my friends, acquaintances—strangers for that matter—have read *Gift from the Sea*, even cherished it, yet cannot find time for solitude each day. Each *day*?! Most of us cannot find time for solitude each year, each decade . . . some of us sadly, never find it in a lifetime. Why, I wonder?

Why did it take *me* so long to make time and space for solitude in my life? I guess that is the question I need to answer . . . so I don't ever stay away from myself for so long again.

Still, I have so many questions and so few answers. My editor gently insists, "I don't want answers, tell me about your process." She is right. We all have to find our own answers. That is why I *Return to the Sea*. Again and again.

— *Anne M. Johnson*

Return to the Sea

*T*his afternoon I sat in one of the cubby-
holes and looked for a long time at the sea
. . . Foam is so beautiful and so manifold
in its beauty and so transient. And as always, there are no words, no means of
satisfying that feeling "Verweile doch,
du bist so schön.*" *****

---

* Quotation from Goethe's *Faust*: "Abide with me, you are so fair."
** From *Bring Me a Unicorn: Diaries and Letters of Anne Morrow Lindbergh 1922-1928.*

Return to the Sea

*H*ave you read it?" my friend Anna asked me in passing, as she noticed my gaze fall upon the book lying on her coffee table. "Elizabeth gave it to me for Christmas. She says she reads it once a year. Have you read it?" Anna asked again.

Gift from the Sea by Anne Morrow Lindbergh. A resplendent new edition. It took me by surprise. Had I read it? Had I *read* it?! No, I don't think I would say I had merely read it. I had *breathed* it. I had drawn life from it. I had wrapped myself up in it like an unborn child nestled in a mother's womb.

Seeing it again after so many years suddenly made me feel like a child. A lost child. A found-lost child. One who had suddenly stumbled into her mother after being separated in a huge department store for what felt like a thousand life times. Even though I knew everything would be fine now that I was no longer lost, I felt like crying. But I was too big to cry, too big to run into my mother's arms and say, *Hold me, make me safe again, keep me safe for always.*

"Yes, I've read it." I told Anna nonchalantly. I can be a great actress when I want to be. Taking a deep breath, I changed the subject casually, as though the book hadn't just unleashed a torrent of emotions within me. I remained poised on the outside, but inside, I was already counting the days, the hours, the minutes until I would be in my own home again, alone, with the girls back in school after the holiday break. Then I would find my old copy of *Gift from the Sea.*

It was days later that I was able to look for my book. A wintry day, just after the first of the year. My Springer spaniel and black cat were curled up in the warm morning sun that streamed in through the kitchen windows onto the wooden floor. I walked right by the mess in the sink and on the counter. Not an easy thing for me to do. I went downstairs and began to peruse the bookshelves. When I couldn't find it right away, I began to feel panicky.

I couldn't have lost it? Could I? Did I give my copy away to someone?

But then, there it was, warped and yellowed, sandwiched in between an ancient collection of paperback novels. Finally, my eyes fell upon the familiar and well-worn jacket of my once-beloved copy of Anne Morrow Lindbergh's masterpiece *Gift from the Sea.* Unpretentious. As if patiently waiting for my inevitable return.

In a way, finding it was like coming across an old

diary. Every dog-eared page, underlined sentence, and note in the margin was evidence of the personal triumph or struggle I had been going through at the time I had made my mark. A change in penmanship, a different color ink—these subtle details signaled the particular stage of life I was in when I left the notations behind years ago.

I easily recognized my teen-aged self in the bold underlines and confident remarks (big loopy letters, blue ink). *YES, this all makes sense, this is how I will order my life! Always allow time for contemplation and creativity! I will always be in touch with my center! Of course I will be a successful spouse, mother, career person, community member while still living in harmony with myself and God. Anne Morrow Lindbergh's goals are my goals. Her shells with their insightful gifts will give me guidance.*

The straight and sure underlines of my youth gradually turned into question marks with the passing of years . . . faint, hesitant pencil marks. Tracing the soft lead lines with my finger, I felt a deep sense of compassion for the busy young wife, mother, and professional I had been when I entered them. Each question mark was like a silent cry from my heart. Why were the gifts of sea—contentment and serenity—still eluding me?

As a young woman determined to follow Anne Lindbergh's example, I had made time to get away once in a while. I had lived very simply by most people's standards. I was highly committed to my marriage. I found an outlet for my creativity in the school I started for my children and the teaching I did at the local college. I was active in my church. I put my energy into attempts to improve myself in order to live gracefully from my center.

Yet I didn't have much inner peace to show for it. Once I put *Gift from the Sea* down and took up the demands of life with a spouse, three small children, a house, and job, I quickly became crabby and dissatisfied. Falling short of my ideals, I began to criticize myself for what I assumed was my incompetence.

Were inner peace and union with God unrealistic expectations? Was I merely setting myself up for the inevitable crash and self-recrimination that always awaited me when, back in the mainstream of my life, any contentment I cultivated in times by myself flew out the door as soon as I opened it to run errands, walk the dog, get the children to school and myself to work on time? Painfully penciled-in question marks.

It was probably sometime in my late twenties that I put *Gift from the Sea* back on the shelf for the last time. I put it away, thinking it had given me false hopes. I hadn't found what I was looking for, what in my teenage years I had been so certain was within my reach: a way to live creatively and contentedly, in harmony with God and myself. *Gift from the Sea* had been something to entice myself with when I was an optimistic teenager; it had been a source of encouragement when I first stepped into the roles of wife, mother, and career woman. But in the end, I had not found a map to the inner peace I was looking for.

Or maybe I had.

Was the guidance I needed right there all along, between the front and back cover of my torn and tattered edition, "published in 1955," the one I had left to gather dust on the shelf? Could it be I simply didn't have the eyes to see what I needed to see in years past?

I longed to crawl back into the lap of *Gift from the Sea.* I wanted to curl up inside its pages so I could feel safe and warm, like I once did when I believed I could live the life Anne Morrow Lindbergh prescribed by just willing it to be so. But part of me was afraid to approach her words again. Had I outgrown them forever? Instead of lending comfort, would her words cause me to dissolve into a puddle of tears and regret for years lost, years I had spent ignoring the wisdom available right there beside me on my night stand?

My heart beat harder and my hands trembled with anticipation as I prepared myself to read *Gift from the Sea* once more. I felt like a prodigal child as I stared at the first page, a child who had left the nest in order to find and experience her own truth. Now I was returning home. What would I find waiting for me—open arms or a closed door?

Whatever it was that awaited me, it was time to face it. In my heart of hearts, I knew it was time to return to the sea.

... *going deeper* ...

☺ Consider reading *Gift from the Sea* slowly.

If you've read it as a younger woman, can you recall how it touched you the first time you read it?
And this time? What longings does it give rise to
now?

If this is your first reading of *Gift from the Sea*, what
feelings or longings or inspirations does it invoke?

☺ Note your insights in your journal or talk them
over with a friend.

The
Beach

To me there is something completely and satisfyingly restful in that stretch of sea and sand, sea and sand, sea and sand and sky —complete peace, complete fulfillment.*

The Beach

The beach is not the place to work; to read,
write or think. I should have remembered
that from other years.

As I started to read the opening chapter of *Gift from
the Sea*, "The Beach," I smiled to myself. *As a matter
of fact,* I thought, *I do remember how much a beach is* not *a
place to work or read and think and write . . .*

Along the rocky shores of a spring-fed lake in
Northern Minnesota there is a tiny beach. Not more
than twelve feet long and four feet wide, it's only a
stone's throw from a small cabin that had been in my
husband's family for over three generations.

I used to love to sit beside that beach, on the old
pier that jutted out from the shore. I loved to sit there at
dusk in midsummer when the days were hot and long.
The water was so smooth, like liquid glass. I loved to do
nothing but watch the huge setting sun and towering
green pines that lined the farther shore dance together,
slow and sensual, in the reflection of the water. My

breath and spirit slipped easily into the ebb and flow of
the sultry movement of the tide and became one with
the quiet, lapping waves.

I had decided once that dusk was my favorite
time of day to sit along the shore. The dawn was beautiful, too, that couldn't be denied—always soft and fresh,
mist rising, birds singing. But the morning gave its gentle light away to the bright busyness of day. I loved the
twilight because it gave its glow over silently and completely to the heart.

Often I was alone with my daughters this time
of evening. (The "men" were usually out fishing.) It
filled me with such sweet joy to watch the slender sil-
houettes of my little girls, bending and reaching as they
hunted for agates below the surface of the shallow waters. Tiny squeals of delight would pierce the quiet now
and then, as would the soft "plunk" of a treasure as it
was dropped carefully into their plastic buckets.

I could almost always count on the great blue
heron to make his appearance each night as I kept vigil
on the pier. He would heave his majestic body from
amongst the reeds on the western shore where he fished
all day. Slowly and regally he'd flap his wings as he made
his trek home across the sky. His wings were like magnificent billows, I thought, putting out the last glowing
embers of the fiery hot summer sun, all that remained of
the long, lazy summer day.

The woods began to prepare for sleep as night

fell. Crickets began their chirping. Fireflies dotted the edge of the thicket next to the shore. Then the first light would be turned on in a cabin across the way. A star would appear. The children's laughter faded as they made their way into bed where grandma waited with pj's, story, and snack. A loon would cry. And then the reassuring hum of a quiet motor could be heard as the men returned home safely with their catch.

I always hoped I would die at Smith Lake, like my husband's grandfather who had died with a fish on his line, in his old boat just off the shore where the sunnies like to hide in the cattails. It would be so easy to die there, especially at twilight. The journey would be short; I was already so close to heaven.

Our tiny beach on Smith Lake was serene, far removed from my hectic life as wife, mother, and career woman. But to get to the beach meant I had to pack the bags, rearrange schedules, and travel long distances. It sometimes exhausted me just thinking about all that had to be done to prepare for our summer excursion to Minnesota: *Pay bills before leaving; stop the mail and cancel the paper; ask the neighbors to feed the cats, rabbit, and bird, and water the garden; do laundry; pack rain gear, sunscreen, bug spray, water toys, an electric fan, clothes for warm, hot, and cold weather . . .*

The list never seemed to get any shorter, and I never seemed to start early enough, or give myself enough time, to get it all done in a relaxed fashion.

Anxiety would set in about two days before we were to leave and reached a peak the morning of departure: *Did I remember to do everything: turn the air off, shut the windows, leave instructions about the pets? Will the car make the trip? Did I pack enough snacks and activities to keep the kids busy for the drive? Did I remember to empty out the fridge?* Sometimes I wondered if the peace and quiet I found at the lake were worth all the work it took to get there.

And then one spring, the lake cabin was sold. I felt an incredible heaviness in my heart, as though the most precious thing in my life were being torn from me. I cried. Would I never again know the sweet serenity of Smith Lake at twilight? The deep contentment of my soul at rest? Suddenly, I knew beyond a doubt, it had been worth every ounce of effort to get to Smith Lake each summer. Because it was along her shores that I experienced inner tranquillity.

Evenings on the pier had put me in touch with a still place inside. I had tasted contentment on those rocky shores at dusk each summer. With Smith Lake gone, could I find a place that would never be sold or taken from me? Could I find an inner peace independent of where I was or what I was doing? I wanted to make inner contentment my resource, my companion, not just one week of the year, not just when I found myself in a place far removed from my life as a wife, mother, and career person but in the *middle* of it.

Slowly it began to dawn on me that, to rediscover the peacefulness I had known at Smith Lake, I was going to have to incorporate certain aspects of beach-living into my daily existence. And it was obvious which quality of beach-life was most missing and most needed: rest. That relieving cessation of all work, reading, writing, or thinking. First and foremost, I realized I needed rest for my body and spirit. More rest than I had ever given myself permission to enjoy before, except perhaps on those sacred summer days up at the cabin.

How had I let things get so out of sync in my everyday life? How had I come to neglect such a basic human need as rest? I guess it was easy enough to let it happen with three small children, a job, and house to tend, as well as a marriage. Slowly and steadily I had let myself neglect my most basic needs. I rarely got all the sleep I required. I rarely ate three healthful meals each day in a leisurely and relaxed fashion. I never exercised. And I seldom found time for simple pleasures: a walk in the woods, an evening gazing at the stars, an hour absorbed in my favorite music. These things were available to me every day. Why did I think I had to wait until I drove four hundred miles once a year to Northern Minnesota to enjoy them?

For many years, I used the excuse of a shortage of time and an abundance of responsibilities as reasons for denying myself basic nurturing. There was always a good and noble reason why I didn't have the time to attend to my own needs. But if I was truly honest with myself, "having time" was never the real issue. The truth was I had begun to believe that making time for myself was less important than paying the bills, cleaning the house, or meeting a deadline. "Indulging" in rest was just that—an indulgence, selfish and irresponsible, appropriate only on rare occasions, like summer holidays. I had come to base my self-worth on the number of things I could get done in a timely fashion. If I left things undone while I relaxed, I was a failure of some sort. So I kept on "doing."

Not taking care of myself eventually caught up with me. I hadn't slipped into drugs, alcohol, overspending, or overeating, but I had slipped into a destructive habit nonetheless. I had gotten into the habit of thinking I would find rest and serenity *just as soon as* I made sure everything and everybody in my life was taken care of. Unfortunately, that never came to pass; I could always find just one more task that needed my attention.

Finally, I simply ran out of gas. I was exhausted physically, emotionally, and spiritually. I couldn't use the excuses anymore; I couldn't justify not caring for myself any longer. I had reached a point where I was too depleted to give anything of myself to anyone. And I couldn't hide it. I cried or lost my temper at the drop of a hat. I had dark circles under my eyes. The small of my back was so tense at night it would begin to spasm. I had a hard time sleeping. And when I did sleep, I slept with my hands clenched so tightly in a fist that my arms ached in the morning. I couldn't "do" anymore. My body was giving me a wake-up call. Thank God, I was forced to listen.

Gradually, still somewhat reluctantly, I began paying attention to my basic human needs. As much as I knew it was what I needed to do, as much as it felt wonderful to begin taking care of myself, a part of me kept dragging its heels. Why was it so difficult to treat myself kindly? Obviously it was good for me. It was unreasonable to think I could deny myself tender loving care and still live in harmony with myself and God. I didn't treat my husband or children this way. I didn't think they could go without good food, rest, and play and still be happy. I made sure they got plenty of whatever it was they needed. So why was I so hard on myself? Where had I learned that making time for myself was unimportant? What did I gain by trying to hang on to this false belief?

When I finally started taking care of my own needs (and it is something I still need to remind myself to do, though it gets easier and more natural every year), I discovered what set me off on the path to self-denial in the first place. It wasn't the demands of a house, the kids, or my job. It wasn't a shortage of time and an abundance of responsibilities, as I had fooled myself into believing for so long. It was my mind-set.

Four hundred miles didn't stand between me

and inner peace; my mind did. Traversing *its* terrain would make seven hours in a station wagon packed to the hilt with luggage, three kids under age five, a husband, and Springer spaniel on a hot and humid August day, with no air-conditioning, seem like a piece of cake.

But the sea was calling me. I *had* to find my way to the beach. Not to the beach of some remote island, not even to the beach of my beloved Smith Lake. I needed to make the journey back to the beach of my heart.

... *going deeper* ...

⊚ Take time to review your needs. Start with the most basic:
Do you get enough sleep?
Do you eat nutritious foods at regular times?
Do you take time to sit down and eat leisurely?
Do you get enough exercise?
Do you do things that are purely for enjoyment to nourish your soul and expand your life?

⊚ Pick one basic need to pay attention to this week. Make a commitment to be kind to yourself in this area for the next seven days. Be patient. Don't judge yourself.

If you want to focus on getting more sleep ...
Consider being kind to yourself by going to bed at a time each night that will allow you to feel replenished by rest. Consider a warm bath, a foot massage with oil, or aromatherapy at bedtime. If you watch television in the evening, consider eliminating some TV time to allow for more time of pure rest.

If you want to focus on eating better ...
Begin to notice when you are hungry and what

you really need to eat. Give yourself permission to spend time enjoying your food. Consider keeping plenty of fresh fruits and vegetables and wonderful whole grain breads and pastas on hand so when you feel hungry you can eat healthful delights.

If you want to focus on getting more exercise . . .
Review the activities for your week ahead. Schedule one-half hour three times this week when you can take a leisurely walk, stretch, practice hatha yoga, swim, or do some kind of exercise that will nourish your body.

If you want to nourish your soul . . .
Consider setting aside some time each day to do something for pure enjoyment, something that is expansive. Listen to music, sing, laugh, talk with a friend, enjoy nature, draw, paint, read something inspiring.

   Note in your journal how your steps toward taking better care of yourself affect you and those around you.

Channelled
Whelk

But life itself is always pulling you away from the understanding of life.*

* From *War Within and Without: Diaries and Letters of Anne Morrow Lindbergh 1939-1944.*

Channelled Whelk

The shell in my hand is deserted. It once housed a whelk, a snail-like creature, and then temporarily, after the death of the first occupant, a little hermit crab, who has run away, leaving his tracks behind him like a delicate vine on the sand. He ran away, and left me his shell. It was once a protection to him. I turn the shell in my hand, gazing into the wide open door from which he made his exit. Had it become an encumbrance? Why did he run away? Did he hope to find a better home? A better mode of living?

I think I could read this paragraph a hundred times, and it would still evoke the same strong feelings of empathy in me. I have such fond and tender feelings for the hermit crab that scurried away from his home, leaving this channelled whelk shell behind. I think we are kindred spirits, this little creature and I, both of us intimately familiar with the persistent desire to find a home that is less confining, a shelter that gives us more room to grow, more space to breathe. Both of us have that inner urge to move on, to continually pursue a way of life that allows for greater freedom and fulfillment. Both of us have left empty shells behind.

Many times in the years since my last reading of *Gift from the Sea*, I've wished I were as lucky as the hermit crab, lucky enough to simply up and crawl away. Lucky enough to shed the external trappings of my existence, to leave behind the complexities and demands of my everyday living space and pace with no regrets, no remorse, no looking back over my shoulder. Many times in the past, I've thought to myself, *If only I could simply unload the burdens and responsibilities of my life, then I would be truly free—free to live in harmony with God and myself.*

Many days I've longed to live lightly, surrounded only by what is absolutely necessary—or absolutely beautiful. Anne Morrow Lindbergh likened her island home to the whelk shell because of its airy simplicity. As I read her description of this living space, I am overcome by a wistful sort of envy. I've often daydreamed of living in an utterly pristine environment—one with bare floors, open windows, and sparse furnishings. A useful and simple wooden chair and table, bed and handmade quilt, a spattering of old and cracked mismatched dishes, rich in personality if lacking in perfection. And then, just to please the eye, nose, and spirit, a bouquet of freshly picked wildflowers overflowing from a mason jar poised upon a small desk. A spray of autumn leaves and pine cones gently resting in a basket nestled in a quiet corner . . .

. . . I am back at Smith Lake again. I am wandering off from my life, trying to find an escape on some distant shore, in a remote and rustic cabin—in a shell other than my own. I began noticing that I craved open, unencumbered spaces most when I was surrounded by all the clutter. Dirty socks on the floor, dishes piled high in the sink, wet towels tossed in the tub, beds unmade, and kids' collectibles crammed everywhere. *No wonder I'm prone to crabbiness and yearn to scuttle off!* I'd argue in my own defense. *Who wouldn't be, living in such a mess!*

For better or worse, I was never in the position to scurry across the sandy beach into a more spacious, uninhabited shelter as the hermit crab so freely does when its quarters start feeling cramped. I thought my only recourse was to bark orders at my husband and kids to "clean up this mess." Then I'd roll up my sleeves and begin the never-ending, thankless task of straightening up, fussing and fuming all the while, muttering resentfully about the many responsibilities a house and family entail.

I'd pick up piles, clean off counters, sort through stuff in a misguided effort to find the contentment I'd temporarily misplaced, the serenity that had slipped away. Wearily, I'd hunt for my lost center that I mistakenly presumed was buried beneath heaps of house clutter somewhere. Momentarily, it was easy to convince myself that a clean and tidy house was all I needed in order to return to a sense of balance.

But when the house was clean, I would still feel dissatisfied. Contentment would remain evasive even after the house was organized. Exhausted and confused, feeling like a perpetual nag, I'd tell myself there must be a logical explanation for this. Perhaps my discontent was the result of a cluttered house *and a cluttered calendar*. That's it! *I will find serenity,* I told myself more than once, *just as soon as my calendar is as clear as my countertops.*

Imagine! Pure blank calendar pages, nothing on them but wide-open squares, expansiveness interrupted only by the tiny, crisp date precisely printed in each upper-right hand corner. No scribbles, reminders, or commitments! Just long, leisurely expanses of days, weeks, months, and more months with no indication of anything I *have* to do. Open and empty spaces waiting to be filled in with whatever I feel like doing—even if it's nothing at all. Nirvana.

Simple surroundings and a simple schedule. Desperately, I tried to make this the answer to my deep yearning for a sense of harmony with God and myself. Desperately, I hoped this was the path that would lead me back to the beach of my heart.

But it wasn't.

At least not entirely.

*Simplification of outward life is not enough
... This is only a technique, a road to grace.*

As a wife, a mother, and a career person, responsibilities are the name of the game. I have three children and as many pets under my roof. Clutter is a way of life for me. Herding kids here, there, and everywhere is part of the fabric of daily existence. Eliminating the external clutter of my life was not only impractical, it was impossible.

Distraction is, always has been, and probably always will be, inherent in woman's life.

No sooner would I clean up one room then another would become a mess. The minute I scratched one commitment off my calendar, two more would pop up. And pining away for a simpler life only added to my level of frustration, to my inner clutter.

My *inner* clutter.

Why hadn't I noticed this long ago? Why did it take me so long to realize it was my *inner* house that needed cleaning? That it was the clutter *inside* that was the source of my discontent?

Anne Morrow Lindbergh had already told me that simplification of my home and schedule was not enough, but I had to learn the hard way. It took a head-on collision with grace for me to wake up and realize what it was that needed my attention; what it was that I needed to simplify in order to find the inner peace I was looking for.

It was a misty weekday morning. I had been thinking about a sticky situation that was developing at my children's school. I was bothered by the way a particular teacher handled the feelings of the children in his class, and I was wondering how some of the other parents felt about his approach . . .

Maybe I should bring it up with someone. But who? Come to think of it, I don't approve of most people's parenting styles. I wonder why so many people are inept at dealing with emotions? That reminds me, I still have a couple of chapters left to read in that parenting book I started last night. I'd better finish it today so I'm well prepared for my parenting lecture tomorrow. But when? I have a 7:00 o'clock meeting tonight at school, and I have to go grocery shopping. I wonder how much money is in the checking account? Let's see, I paid bills on Saturday, the checks may have all cleared. I'd better play it safe and use cash today. I think I have enough to cover what we absolutely need: milk, something for supper, and I think we're out of cereal. If only I could generate a few more clients, things wouldn't get so tight at the end of the month. Four or five more people and, wow, we might even be able to swing a new car.

Ooops . . . I almost forgot, I need to fit in an oil change some-time soon . . . OH MY GOSH, WHERE AM I?
All of a sudden I realized I was behind the wheel of my car going sixty-five miles an hour down the interstate without a clue as to where I was or where I had been for the last ten minutes or so. In a split second I was jerked out of my thoughts. It happened so fast, I had the sensation of being in two places at one time. Part of me was still thinking thought after thought, while another part of me was suddenly watching my thoughts. And they were whizzing by almost as fast as the scenes outside my windshield.

A rush of adrenaline surged through my body. Quickly I glanced to my right and then in my rear view mirror. All ten (yes, ten!) of my carpool kids (I drove a BIG station wagon!) were safe and snug in their seat belts. I broke out in a mild cold sweat as I tried to get my bearings. Had I missed the exit? Was I still headed east toward the city or had I already made my turnoff toward the kids' school? A sign overhead assured me I was going in the right direction. The blood drained from my limbs, and I felt my knees go weak. Thank goodness I hadn't had an accident or detoured toward Chicago. I took a deep breath and slowly let out a sigh.

I had been lucky this time. But what was I thinking—letting my attention stray so far from the road in front of me? Plain and simple, I had to admit to myself that, from the time I had left the parking lot

where I picked up the kids to the time when I was star-
tled back into the present moment, my mind had spun
an incredible web of worries and judgments, fears and
fantasies. So entangled had I become in the web, I had
lost track of what was going on around me.

> *What a circus act we women perform every*
> *day of our lives. It puts the trapeze artist to*
> *shame. Look at us. We run a tight rope*
> *daily, balancing a pile of books on the head.*
> *Baby-carriage, parasol, kitchen chair, still*
> *under control. Steady now!*

> *This is not the life of simplicity but the life of*
> *multiplicity . . . It leads not to unification*
> *but to fragmentation. It does not bring*
> *grace; it destroys the soul.*

I knew, deep down inside, this wasn't the first
time my thoughts had distracted me away from the
present reality. Was my spiritual well-being courting
disaster as surely as my car had been moments ago? I
winced as I wondered, *Just how much of the beauty of my life*
have I missed because I am preoccupied? Before I had time to
calculate the sad and somewhat embarrassing answer,
another startling question surfaced: *How many of my pre-*
dominant feelings and actions—the very fabric of my life—are
woven out of reactions to hypothetical ideas that I spin out of the

preoccupations of my mind rather than the reality of the situation? How many of my relationships are based on projections rather than honest intimacy?

I cringed.

It wasn't just my house and my schedule that needed simplifying. It was my mind. My mind had become so cluttered with worries and judgments, I couldn't see my way clear to my heart. There could be no denying it. My thoughts detained me in my head, lured me away from my heart. My self-recriminating spiral of thoughts had become an incredible distraction. They constantly pulled me out of the here-and-now. Quite possibly they were leading me down the path of spiritual decline. But which thoughts could I drop? They all seemed equally important. And if I didn't constantly analyze my life and my problems, how could I stay on top of things?

I hadn't a clue how to rein in all the wild horses my thoughts had become. So why even try? I felt much safer cloaked in the protective shell of my ruminations than risking the possibility of losing control of my life. *I'll just be more careful driving from now on,* I vowed.

But it just wasn't that easy to dismiss the car experience. It had unnerved me, shaken something loose inside me. In the days that followed, I found myself observing the incessant chatter in my mind. Old negative thoughts kept spinning round and round: *I am inadequate; I am a failure; I have done so many things wrong; there*

are so many things I need to fix or take care of. I hadn't realized I had so many negative judgments and opinions
about myself.

The more I noticed my thoughts, the louder
they boomed. Being inside my head was like being
caught in an echo chamber. I wanted to crawl outside of
myself. I wanted to run far, far away from my thoughts.
Like the hermit crab, I longed for a wide open door from
which to make my exit.

Finally, something inside of me cracked. It was
as though a dam had burst inside my head. The shell of
my thoughts that I had built up over the years, trying to
hold back all my deepest fears about myself, shattered
into fragments. I felt myself shriveling up, recoiling
from cold, dark waters that engulfed me. I felt trapped
in the collapsed shell of my own making, drowning in
my own thoughts.

In the past, I had tried to escape my negative
thoughts by crawling from one shell to another. I had
sought refuge in shells called Successful Career Woman,
Champion of Noble Causes, Super-Mom, Wonderful
Wife, Expert in Self-Improvement. If I kept myself busy
doing praiseworthy things, and doing them well, I gave
my mind just cause to generate positive thoughts about
myself. But constantly doing, doing, doing had eventually been my undoing. It wore me out—made me irrita-
ble and cranky—which in turn made me feel guilty and
a failure.

And each time I felt like a failure, I would try to shed my shell and exchange it for a more attractive one, one in which I could hide my inadequacies. But in the end, none of the shells I ran to could protect me from self-contempt. Now I understood why. There was no place far enough to run and hide where my negative thoughts could not find me. My thoughts went wherever I went.

It was a painful time. I was stripped of the heavy encrustation that had served as my protection for so long. My false shell—the part of me that drove me to fix, improve, make myself and my life "perfect"—was being crushed. I felt as if I were losing my identity. This shell was the only "me" I knew. The only "me" I thought honorable and worth perpetuating. And now it seemed worthless, a sham. I no longer had the will to push for perfection. I surrendered.

I remember looking at my three beautiful daughters and feeling nothing. I remember looking into the eyes of the husband I loved and feeling nothing. I went about my daily duties removed, unfeeling. But now there was no background chatter. I had run out of thoughts. I didn't seem to care enough about the past, present, or future to generate any new thoughts. I surmised that, like the whelk, like the hermit crab, like every creature that crawls around the earth incessantly scuttling after illusive happiness, I would eventually shrivel up and die in my shell.

I had never allowed myself to surrender so completely before, to free fall, so I had no way of knowing there actually was a bottom to this emotional pit. Not a soft, plush landing . . . but not an obliterating cement floor either. Just a release, something like the space at the end of an exhale—an expanse that dissolves into the ethers and then you have to breathe in again.

And just as I was catching my breath, I was caught unawares again.

It was an overcast afternoon of what had become a typical day for me. I trudged along listlessly, completing with very little, if any, interest whatever mundane task happened to lie in front of me. On this particular day, it was the bathroom that needed my attention. After scouring the sink and toilet, I knelt down to scrub the tub. First, I needed to clean the hair out of the drain, a job that usually nauseated me. I reached over the porcelain edge and began to unscrew the plug. As I started to perform one of the most distasteful household duties imaginable, I suddenly felt a tiny, cool, trickling spring of something bubbling up from my heart, a feeling I couldn't immediately name. A childhood memory of a thunderstorm on a hot summer day flashed through me. I remembered the feel of rain spilling from the roof tops, dripping on my head and slithering down my spine as I stood, clad in my swimsuit under the eaves of our house after a storm, completely open and receptive to nature's sensuous, soothing pleasure.

I was so astonished by this spontaneous sensation awakening inside of me, I dropped my sponge and cleanser, abandoned the task at hand, and sat back on my legs to relish every delicious minute of it. I hadn't felt anything in days, and nothing remotely like this in . . . well, in, I didn't know how long. I began to search for a name to call this feeling, but the name arose of its own accord: joy.

I started to weep and laugh all at once. This spontaneous joy certainly wasn't caused by anyone or anything outside of me. For heaven's sake, I was cleaning the hair out of the tub when it erupted, thinking about nothing at all! This newfound joy was coming from a space deep inside of me; it was coming from the depths of my heart.

Grace shows up in the oddest of places—in a '77 Chevy wagon and a hair-clogged drain. I was alive again.

The final answer, I know, is always inside.

I began to understand the reason why I was so often discontented. Somewhere along the way I'd mistakenly accepted the false notion that joy was dependent on external circumstances. Like most people, I believed things outside of myself "made me happy." An evening on the pier at the lake "made me happy." My children, when they were well behaved, "made me happy." My husband, when things were going well between us, "made me happy." People's good opinion of me "made me happy." This subtle but powerful belief had been reinforced over and over again by society and by my own experience. I was, after all, temporarily and superficially happy when things went my way.

But things didn't always go my way. Eventually the tide would turn, and then, if what I needed in order to be happy lay "out there," it followed that I had to chase after it and hold on tight once I got it. No wonder I was always so exhausted! Happiness was always a "when." When the bills were paid, when I got my degree, got the baby out of diapers, got my daughter through adolescence, when I lost ten pounds, when I could get my husband to help out around the house more . . . then I'd be happy. Contentment—that state of satisfaction I had experienced on the pier at twilight —was always just one-problem-to-be-solved away.

I'd convinced myself that my efforts to be responsible and conscientious would be rewarded with inner contentment. I couldn't have been farther from the truth. Anne Morrow Lindbergh warns us of the dangers of trying so hard. She called it "digging":

The sea does not reward those who are
too anxious,
too greedy,
or too impatient.

To dig for treasures shows
not only impatience and greed,
but lack of faith.

All the while I was responsibly crossing one more "to-do" off my never-ending lists, my life was steadily becoming a cumbersome shell I felt a desperate desire to escape from. I found myself constantly wishing I could "get away for a while" from all this "pursuit of happiness" so that I could find what I was longing for— deep inner joy.

The kind of joy that begins as a trickle, and then erupts like a geyser, right in the middle of scrubbing the tub.

I had been looking in the wrong direction for contentment. When I felt disgruntled and edgy, out of sorts and dissatisfied with my life, I thought it was the result of not having something: the right job, enough money, a cleaner house, a better schedule. I was always looking for contentment outside of myself, in someone, something, or some perfect set of circumstances. But, all along, my discontent was the result of not being aware of, and connected to, what I already had as a source of joy and contentment, residing deep within my heart.

Now that I had a taste of the serenity I had been looking for, for so long, I wanted more. I wanted to learn how I could hold onto it, how I could sustain it, how I could return to the beach of my heart whenever I needed to.

The lesson of the channeled whelk resounded in my heart once again: simplify.

One learns first of all in beach living the art of shedding; how little one can get along with, not how much.

I can tell when it's time to start "shedding" when I notice my mind racing. When my breathing becomes shallow and my body becomes tense. When I feel like lashing out at someone or something. When I start doing something compulsively, such as frantically cleaning the house, lecturing my children, or becoming defensive in a discussion with my spouse. Then I know it's time to retreat to my inner island space.

I think of this inner space as "the witness" place, a place where I can observe my thoughts without judgment or attachment. A place where I can become aware of what is going on in my head and how it is affecting me. A place where I can get a clearer perspective.

For instance, when my thoughts are racing about the mess my house is in, if I remember to slow down and become the witness, I can notice that my thoughts are saying things like, *I am exhausted and I'll never get all this housework done. I am sick and tired of cleaning. I'd rather sit by the fire and read a good book. But if I don't do the cleaning, no one will. How do other women do it? I only work part-time, and I can't keep up the house. I should just try harder.*

By stepping back from my thoughts for a moment, observing them, and listening carefully to the feelings behind them, I can respond to the truth that exists in them: *I am exhausted.* I probably do need to rest! Put my feet up. Respond to what my body and spirit is asking for.

By observing my thoughts, I can also discover which ones aren't based on reality: *If I don't clean, no one will.* How do I know? Have I asked anyone to help? Or am I assuming this, projecting my fears and doubts onto the situation, creating a self-fulfilling prophesy? My family has always pitched in and helped in the past, when I've given them a chance by asking.

From this witness perspective I am able to see which thoughts I ought to discard, shed entirely: *How do other women do it? I only work part-time, and I can't keep a house clean.* I am not *other* women; I am *me*. Comparing myself to others only pulls me out of my heart and into my head where I find criticisms instead of compassion. When I can witness without criticism, I can see that my mind is filled with unrealistic expectations: *I should try harder.* I can respect that I have needs, limitations. My worth is not based on what I do.

This witness space is like Anne Morrow Lindbergh's island. It is a place where I can remove myself from my usual preoccupations. It is a place of detachment where I can slow down and observe. From this place, I can more clearly see what thoughts serve me well and which thoughts are merely habitual and weigh me down. When I take time to retreat to the witness space, I find myself on the beach of my heart. This journey to the beach doesn't take planning and packing, but it does take practice. One thing I find helpful is to watch my breathing. I start by reminding myself to take a few deep, cleansing breaths. A long breath in and a slow breath out, a long breath in and a slow breath out. Then, I let myself listen to what my thoughts are saying. Sometimes I simply verbalize my thoughts, or journal them. This helps me become clearer about what I am feeling, so I can ask for what I need or give myself what I am in need of. Often, a sense of calm replaces my agitation or worry. A feeling of empathy for myself, or for the person I am interacting with or thinking about, replaces my harsh judgments. I thank myself. I thank my thoughts for having sent up a "red flag" that serves as a reminder to turn within—to the quiet shores of my heart, to a place where "the wind, the sun, the smell of the pines" can blow freely on bare floors and sparse furnishing.

> *One is free, like the hermit crab, to change one's shell.*

By grace I had stumbled upon an ancient truth: when I embrace the invitation to "be still and know that I am God," I *can* change my shell, my life . . . from the inside out.

... *going deeper* ...

☺ Over the course of the next few days, set aside some intentional time to "witness" your thoughts. Just watch them. Notice the amount of chatter in your mind. Consider which thoughts you might want to shed. Ask for Divine guidance in devising an inner "housecleaning" plan that you feel comfortable with. Jot down your ideas in your journal.

☺ Invite yourself to consider any nagging concern that may need your attention. Is there a situation that is causing you emotional or spiritual pain? Be compassionate with yourself. Remember that caring for yourself means asking for help when you need it. There are people—friends and professionals—who can help you take the steps to rediscover balance and harmony in your life. The first step is to become aware and honest about what needs your attention.

☺ Reflect on these questions: Is there something I am chasing after in life? Have I been running from shell to shell trying to find it? Has that worked? Where do I think what I am looking for really resides? Use your journal to record your reflections.

◎ Set some time aside to think about a person, place, or situation that brings you great joy. Close your eyes and get a clear image of this person or situation. Let yourself feel the love, joy, and happiness that arises as you think about what gives you so much satisfaction. Once you are deeply immersed in that joy, let go of the image of that which you thought "gave you" these feelings of love and happiness. Recognize that the love you feel comes from inside of you, it is not coming from anything outside of yourself. Let yourself bask in your inner bliss.

◎ During this week, pay special attention to times when you experience small joys—as you watch your child sleep, gaze into the eyes of one you love, hear some good news, receive a heartfelt thank you. Slow down enough to relish the inner experience, become familiar with it.

Moon Shell

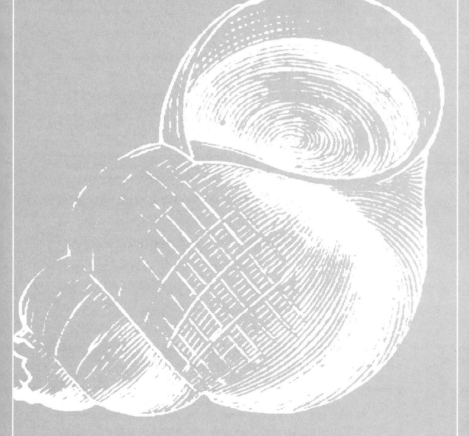

People talk about love as though it were something you could give, like an armful of flowers. And a lot of people give love like that—just dump it down on top of you, a useless strong-scented burden. I don't think it is anything that you can give . . . Love is a force in you that enables you to give other things. It is the motivating power. It enables you to give strength and power and freedom and peace to another person. It is not a result; it is a cause. It is not a product; it produces. It is a power . . . It has taken me a long time to learn. I hope it will stay learned and that I can practice it.*

* From *Locked Rooms and Open Doors: Diaries and Letters of Anne Morrow Lindbergh 1933-1935*.

Moon Shell

*This is a snail shell, round, full and glossy as
a horse chestnut. Comfortable and compact,
it sits curled up like a cat in the hollow of my
hand. Milky and opaque, it has the pinkish
bloom of the sky on a summer evening, rip-
ening to rain. On its smooth symmetrical
face is penciled with precision a perfect spiral, winding inward to the pinpoint center
of the shell, the tiny dark core of the apex,
the pupil of the eye. It stares at me, this mys-
terious single eye—and I stare back.*

*Now it is the moon, solitary in the sky, full
and round, replete with power . . . Now it
is an island, set in ever-widening circles of
waves, alone, self-contained, serene.*

Who am I?" my nine-year-old daughter asked me
one day as she lay soaking in a warm, sudsy tub.

"I'm not my legs, I'm not my arms, I'm not my muscles," she mused, "but *I* make them move. Who am I? I'm not my eyes, I'm not my ears, but *I* see and hear. I'm not my brain, but *I* use it to think. Who am I, Mom? Where am *I* in my body?"

How could I answer such a wise and sage philosopher? After nearly forty years, I was still trying to figure it out. She, the budding existentialist, wanted to know the answer now, at age nine.

In many ways, it seemed as if the older I got, the harder it was to discern who *I* was. I was too busy responding to the cares and concerns of others—my family, friends, clients, and the community—to sort out my own needs and desires, the purpose of my life. Gradually, I had slipped into becoming the roles that I played: wife and mother, counselor, volunteer at church and school.

It wasn't that I didn't enjoy all of the roles that I assumed, because I did. Giving of myself came naturally and gave me a certain sense of satisfaction. Yet deep down inside, I often felt a vague sense of emptiness. It seemed as if I had lost a part of myself in the process of attending to the needs of so many other people.

> *Is this what happens to woman? She wants*
> *perpetually to spill herself away. All her in-*
> *stincts as a woman—the eternal nourisher*
> *of children, of men, of society—demands*

that she give. Her time, her energy, her crea-
tiveness drain out into these channels if there
is any chance, any leak.

My inner emptiness felt like a yearning for completion and fullness, a longing to feel connected to my
core, my inner essence, the real "me." It was an uncom-
fortable feeling, one that made me want to do something: call a friend, read a book, throw myself into a
project that would keep my hands and mind busy. It
surfaced as a kind of restlessness—there had to be more
to life than packing lunches, vacuuming up dog hair, or-
ganizing the pizza sales at school, or even counseling
people with intriguing problems. I attempted to ease
my emptiness by setting new goals for myself and work-
ing hard to reach them. But no matter how much I ac-
complished, that hollow feeling would always return.

No longer fed by a feeling of indispensabil-
ity or purposefulness, we are hungry, and
not knowing what we are hungry for, we
fill up the void with endless distractions, al-
ways at hand—unnecessary errands, com-
pulsive duties, social niceties. And for the
most part, to little purpose. Suddenly the
spring is dry: the well is empty.

I had to admit it. I *was* empty. And I wanted to

fill myself up. I wanted to fill myself up with ME. I wanted there to be enough of me to go around and still have some of me left over for myself. A lot of me, in fact. I didn't want to be stingy with myself, but I didn't want to be exhausted and drained either. I wanted to feel so full of me that I would be able to give generously, without becoming resentful. I wanted to be full—like the moon—*"full and round, replete with power."*

How many nights had I lain awake in my bed, gazing out the window at the nectarean light of the moon, only to wish I knew her secret for shining forth so radiantly? She allowed her light to flow so freely, so abundantly, like mother's milk, to everything below. I wanted to be like that: full and generous, like the moon glowing in the heavens.

But first I had to figure out who *I* was.

If asked the question, "Who are you?" I would have replied, "I am Anne Johnson, formerly Annie Sinsky. I am a tall, average weight woman with curly, red hair. I am a wife, mother, and therapist. I am this person I tote around inside of my body every day. Someone with a particular life history. A personality with thoughts, feelings, hopes, dreams, and fears. I am an individual with strengths and weaknesses. I have my own set of values and beliefs. I think Freud would say, I am the ego, the id, and the superego. That's who I am."

At least, that's what I—and most everyone else raised in Western culture—have been taught to believe.

But ever since that morning I had felt myself split in two while driving the kids to school, when I had come face-to-face with my identity and seen it as somewhat of a shell, an outer layer of protection my mind and imagination had come up with, I couldn't give pat answers any more.

There is the "me" who is currently sitting at the computer typing. But what about the "me" that once was a sleeping newborn or a stubborn two-year-old? What became of the "me" that used to be a pretending four-year-old, a shy and overweight nine-year-old, a dreamy and idealistic thirteen-year-old? Where is that determined and independent seventeen-year-old girl, the confused and depressed twenty-six-year-old woman, the cocky and confident thirty-year-old "me"? Where did all those "me's" go?

How could I uncover the answer to this most basic, yet mystifying, persistent question, *Who am I?*

Solitude, says the moon shell. Every person, especially every woman, should be alone sometime during the year, some part of each week, and each day.

. . . the core, the inner spring, can best be refound through solitude

I wanted to find my core, to embrace it, to nourish it. But I thought I had already ventured down the path of solitude, and I hadn't found myself at the end of the road. I regularly used the quiet time, after the kids were in bed, to be alone with my stack of books on self-help and spirituality in order to discover myself, to figure out just who I was and how I could improve on this year's model of "me." Periodically, I carved out time for myself even when the kids were awake, to have lunch with a friend, to discuss my "issues"—get to know the "real" me. And occasionally, I even spent time completely alone, doing exactly what *I* wanted to do: clean out a closet or a drawer, put all the recent photos into an album, write a few long overdue letters, go for a swim. Weren't these all good examples of spending time in solitude?

Maybe not. Maybe being alone with a friend, or alone with my books, alone with my tasks wasn't all there was to solitude. Even when I was alone, I was never *with only* "me." No wonder I rarely felt in harmony with myself. Steadily, it was occurring to me that I might have the wrong definition for the word. "Solitude" might mean something else, something more, something much more.

Maybe the moon shell held a clue about the journey to solitude: *"winding inward to the pinpoint center of the shell, the tiny dark core of the apex."* If I was going to be with myself I needed to go to my center, to the place inside where I was truly alone and truly quiet.

What a simple but radical concept—to consider that there might be value in simply sitting quietly, alone with myself, entertaining no thoughts whatsoever. My old patterns of thinking argued, *Why sit around with a blank mind? Isn't that a waste of time? If I sit and do nothing, won't I start thinking of everything that needs to get done? Wouldn't it make more sense to just get up and do it? What merit can there be in being completely still, in not doing anything, in not thinking about anything?*

Even if I could rationalize trying to find some time in my hectic schedule for pure, undisturbed peace and quiet—as an experiment, if nothing else, to see what might reveal itself—there was a part of me that was afraid to venture into inner silence.

We seem so frightened today of being alone that we never let it happen . . . We must relearn to be alone.

Yet I knew it was time. Time to follow the path of the moon shell spiraling inward. Time to discover the treasure hidden deep inside, the "I" that could only be experienced in a space along the silent shores of my heart. It seemed simple enough to set aside a few minutes each day to rest in external and internal solitude. But it wasn't. I echoed Anne Morrow Lindbergh's thoughts:

It is a difficult lesson to learn today—to leave one's friends and family and deliberately practice the art of solitude . . . [It] is more a question of inner convictions than of outer pressures.

I had the best of intentions—to begin each day with quiet time—but with getting myself off to work, and the kids off to school, letting the dog out, feeding the cat, putting one load of laundry in, tidying up the kitchen . . . and wanting to sleep in as long as I possibly could each morning, it didn't always happen. Sometimes I had the energy and discipline to get up extra early and sit quietly, undisturbed before my husband's alarm went off, but not often. Usually it was some time in the late afternoon, just before I had to begin fixing dinner, that I noticed I was feeling empty and drained. Instead of identifying that hollow feeling as a need to catch a quick nap or grab a snack, I began to recognize it as my own inner longing to be with myself. It was more typically, then, around dusk that I'd squirrel away in my room, shut the door, turn off the lights, maybe light one small candle, sit down comfortably, and take a few deep breaths.

Finally, a chance to relax. A chance to let go of the tensions of the day. My body gladly cooperated with this process. A few deep breaths was all it took to begin melting the stiffness and tension in my back and neck, the heaviness in my arms and legs.

My mind was another story. It had an agenda of its own. My mind saw this quiet time as a great opportunity to have my undivided attention, a captive audience. It would begin to prattle away, reminding me of things I had to do, problems I had to solve. The more my mind chattered on, the more irritated and agitated I became. Sometimes I would shake my head in disgust, tears would stream down my face, so frustrated was I at my inability to still my mind, to uncover the "me" I was looking for inside.

> *Patience, patience, patience, is what the sea teaches. Patience and faith. One should lie empty, open, choiceless as a beach—waiting for the gift from the sea.*

Patience. Fighting my thoughts was futile. I needed to surrender to the process. I began to think of my thoughts as waves upon the surface of a vast body of water. As they would rise, I would remain detached and watch them ripple out to sea where they would eventually dissolve back into the magnificent waters. As my thoughts dissolved, I could feel and hear the sound of my own breath, like the rise and fall of the tide as it washed up upon the shore.

"*Ham* . . . " I practiced taking a deep breath in. "*Sa* . . . " I let it free . . . There was a distinct coolness to each in-breath, like the breeze off an incoming tide. And with each out-breath there came a soothing warmth, as though the rays of a golden afternoon sun were streaming through my entire being.

At the top of each in-breath and the bottom of each out-breath, I noticed there was a space. A dark, rich, velvety space, like the steady, calm waters deep beneath the surface of the sea. I let myself rest there, undisturbed, peaceful, content, thought and desire-free.

This is the same experience I had those lazy long-ago summer nights as I watched the sun go down at Smith Lake. I was able to slip into the depths of my own heart, to be lulled into inner stillness by the ripple of the waves, and to merge with the underlying stillness inherent in the beauty of nature that surrounded me. This, I am discovering, is what it means to be content. This, I am discovering, is what it means to "be with" my self, my inner essence.

I am still the "me" that is bound by time and space, a unique, albeit fleeting, expression of God's unlimited creativity. I still have my own peculiar set of quirks, my own personality, my own struggles and triumphs. I am still tall, average weight, my hair is curly, red, now slightly graying. But I no longer define myself as only this. I am learning there is a timeless, ageless me that lives within my heart, an unbounded "I" that lives in unity with God in The Sea of Inner Stillness.

And what about the moon's secret—the one I

had lain awake nights trying to discover? It seems so obvious now. The secret to the moon's ability to bestow her light so generously on others, while remaining "full and round, replete with power," is that her light is not hers alone. It is a radiant reflection of the sun who, like the divine Light in my heart, is sometimes hidden, but never gone.

> *. . . there is a quality to being alone that is incredibly precious. Life rushes back into the void, richer, more vivid, fuller than before . . . one is whole again, complete and round—more whole, even, than before, when the other people had pieces of one . . .*

> *The problem is . . . how to still the soul in the midst of its activities.*

Now, if while I'm putting my children to bed, I catch myself reciting a litany of chores I have left to do in my head, I slow my breath down, let go of the company of my thoughts, and feel present to the moment. When I remember to do this, my experience is transformed. Instead of being agitated and anxious to get going, I sink into the softness of the moment. I feel the tenderness of my daughter's cheek as I gently caress her skin. I notice the rise and fall of her chest, and hear the wisp of her small breath as she slips into sleep. Love wells up inside of me, sweet gratitude for the precious gift of life. Who are you, dear little daughter of mine? I believe you are a sparkling and unique manifestation of God's love and light. I believe you are one with the stillness that shimmers in your heart. You are one with the creative energy, the life source of the entire universe. But in the end, only you can know the answer to your question, *Who am I?* And I trust you will find that answer, in your own time and in your own way, just as I am finding my answer in my own way.

. . . *going deeper* . . .

◎ Let yourself get a mental image of the "you" of ten years ago. What did you look like? What kind of clothes did you wear? What were your interests, who were the people you spent time with? Then picture the "you" of fifteen years ago, twenty years ago, and so on. In your journal, reflect on the "you" that is present in each image and is present now.

◎ For the next week, begin or end your day with a few moments of solitude. Here are some suggestions that might help you break through the barrier of the "temporary you's" inside shouting for attention:

Chose a place to sit where you won't be disturbed or distracted by the phone or people coming and going. Choose a place that is warm and comfortable. If you choose to sit in a chair, place your feet flat on the floor. If you are seated on the floor, sit in a comfortable cross-legged position.

Place your hands on your lap gently folded. Sit upright, but relaxed. You may want to set an alarm for the amount of time you have so you won't worry about watching the clock. Close your eyes and focus your thoughts on something you love, something or someone that brings you joy and happiness. Feel the happiness and joy warm your heart. Take a few deep cleansing breaths and then let your breathing return to normal. Let the warmth spread to any part of your body where you feel tension. Let your mind become quiet.

If thoughts arise, imagine them to be little sail boats floating on the surface of the water. Just watch each one as it sails by carried by the gentle breezes. There is no need to get involved with your thoughts. Just watch them come and let them go. Feelings may surface from time to time. Tears or laughter. This is fine. Let yourself feel them, and then let them go.

When the amount of time you have allowed for solitude is over, take a few more deep breaths. Slowly open your eyes. Sit quietly for a moment more respecting your inner state. Offer a gesture of gratitude for the time you spent.

Note in your journal the effects these times of solitude have on your experience of life.

Double-Sunrise

*A*nd suddenly I remake an old discovery. It is the striving after perfection that makes one an artist. It is the sense that one is imperfect, unfulfilled, unfinished. One attempts by superhuman effort to fill the gap, to leap over it, to finish it in another medium . . . One must also have glimpsed a vision of perfect[ion] . . . which presses one on . . .*

* From *War Within and Without: Diaries and Letters of Anne Morrow Lindbergh 1939-1944.*

Double-Sunrise

The shell was a gift; I did not find it. It was handed to me by a friend. It is unusual on the island. One does not often come across such a perfect double-sunrise shell. Both halves of this delicate bivalve are exactly matched. Each side, like the wing of a butterfly, is marked with the same pattern; translucent white except for three rosy rays that fan out from the golden hinge binding the two together. I hold two sunrises between my thumb and finger. Smooth, whole, unblemished shell, I wonder how its fragile perfection survived the breakers on the beach.

The perfect double-sunrise shell, almost my nemesis, but in the end, my redemptress. The shell that symbolizes my greatest hurdle in life: to accept "imperfections" as perfectly acceptable . . .

It was a bitter cold night. The wind off the

black, frozen lake outside howled, sending tempera-
tures plummeting far below zero. None of us was looking forward to the long, uphill walk back to our dorm
rooms on the other side of campus. Hoping to postpone
the inevitable, we lingered around the blazing fire that
crackled in the hearth of the church hall where we had
gathered after vespers, fortifying our bodies with dessert
and our morale with lively conversation.

My girlfriend Ruth and I stood off to one side
away from the others, hoping, as usual, to blend into the
woodwork as we abandoned our perpetual diets. We
were devouring chocolate cake with thick fudge frost-
ing, bent over in laughter about something, when
Ruth's boyfriend's roommate, whom I had never met
before, spotted us and came over to ask if we'd like to
play broom ball that winter. Apparently, the church
was forming a team to enter the intramural all-*male*
league and was short a few players. This charmingly
convincing young man wanted to know, "Would we
play?"

Ruth and I were both tall . . . we'd be playing
with helmets on . . . the games were late at night, after
the varsity hockey team was done with practice and the
ice was free for intramural sports . . . in baggy clothes
we could easily pass as men, and the church team *was*
short a few players . . .

"Sure, it sounds like fun," I sputtered. Looking
into the gorgeous blue eyes of our successful and satis-

fied recruiter, I was only a little less than stunned. What had I just committed myself to? I dreaded playing competitive sports, and I had never even heard of broom ball before that moment, much less played it. (Broom ball is a Midwestern sport like hockey, only instead of skates, you wear sneakers on the ice, and instead of using hockey sticks to chase a puck around the rink, you use a broom to smack a deflated volleyball from one end of the field to the other.)

My enthusiasm was fueled by the fact that I knew, right then and there, I had just laid eyes on the man I would marry. Fearlessly, if not a bit foolishly, I figured I'd better start to get to know him, even if it was going to be under such strange circumstances as playing broom ball in an all men's league at the ice shell somewhere close to midnight a couple times a week.

Scott and I were married in less than two years. I was lucky the attractive young man who had asked me to disguise myself as a male broom ball player turned out to be an intelligent, warm, kind, and romantic man, rich in integrity. And he was lucky we won the broom ball championship (in a sudden-death play off at the end of the championship game)! The sun rose and set for me in Scott's eyes. I wanted our love to feel that way forever.

Three years after we were married, Scott was by my side as I gave birth to our first child. After a night of uncomplicated labor, our beautiful daughter was born. Her head crowned precisely at dawn, with the rising summer sun and the sweet song of waking birds. When her warm and wet perfect body was laid upon my breasts, she immediately turned her head of golden curls to look up at me. In that moment, I saw reflected in her eyes a look of complete recognition. I was sure we had always known each other, since the beginning of time. In those first precious moments together, I vowed there would never be anything but love between us.

> *The pure relationship, how beautiful it is!*
> *. . . the first part of every relationship is*
> *pure, whether it be with friend or lover,*
> *husband or child . . . a self-enclosed world*
> *. . . two shells meeting each other, making*
> *one world between them. There are no others*
> *in the perfect unity of that instant, no other*
> *people or things or interests.*

In the course of the next four years, my husband and I had two more darling baby girls. Each daughter's birth elicited the same response from my heart as the first: complete surrender. I was determined to offer nothing short of perfect love to my children and my husband, certain I would receive the same from them in return. I challenged myself to be the perfect mother, the perfect partner, the perfect everything. We would be the perfect family. I wanted my "double-sunrise moments" to span my entire lifetime, with no lulls in between.

In those same four years that we had three babies, we built a house, started our careers, and began paying off student loans from graduate school. At twenty-six years of age, I was up to my ears in job responsibilities, housework, diapers, debt, and disillusionment.

. . . functional relationships tend to take the place of the early all-absorbing personal one.

My husband and I fought. I lost my temper when the kids whined and squabbled. I began to wonder where I had taken a wrong turn. Where did I lose sight of the bliss I had felt in the early stages of my most precious relationships? I wanted it back.

The image of perfection I had created in my mind was too fragile to withstand the realities of life. I saw my double-sunrise shell begin to crumble, and I had no other image to replace it with. Not knowing what else I could do, I tried to pick up the pieces and glue them back together. I tried to create perfection by controlling, fixing, improving—or denying that anything was "broken." I didn't want anyone to experience anger, sadness, disappointment, or conflict. In my mind, these were antithetical to love.

And it was love, after all, that pressed me on toward perfection . . . wasn't it? It was the love I felt for my husband and my children that motivated me to make our lives perfect, or so I thought. Looking back, I can see it was my own yearning to be loved that motivated me. I thought I could "get" love from others . . . if I earned it, if I proved myself worthy of it by doing everything right. Wasn't it love I saw radiating from my partner's and children's eyes when I responded to their needs and wants? I drove myself to be the best at everything I did and then, exhausted, couldn't understand why my efforts weren't rewarded with a life filled with double-sunrise moments.

I began to think maybe it was my husband's fault. That he just didn't appreciate me. That he made unreasonable demands on me to cook, clean, take care of the children, and work a job outside the home. If he would just let up on me, I would be a lot happier and a lot nicer.

But it wasn't Scott who was demanding, criticizing, and judging. It was me. It was me who didn't love myself enough to drop my high expectations, to let up on the demands I placed on myself, to accept myself as "less than perfect." I used Scott as an excuse so I wouldn't have to face up to my own lack of self-love and acceptance, so I wouldn't have to surrender my need to fix and control. That way, I didn't have to muster up the inner courage necessary to do (or not do) what I needed to care for myself.

The temptation is to blame the situation on the other person and to accept the easy solution that a new and more understanding partner will solve everything.

It's easy to distance ourselves, either emotionally or physically, from those we love once they begin to reflect our own inner conflicts, once they begin to disappoint us, or demand things from us we feel we cannot give. It's easy to think that we simply made a wrong choice, that there is someone else, or some other lifestyle out there, that can offer us a life of continuous double-sunrise moments. I know . . . I believed that on more than one occasion. *Many* more than one occasion.

As fate, and life, would have it, those we love most are also those with whom we are destined to spend the most time. They are the ones we become most comfortable with, let our hair down with. Our mate and our children are the ones who see—and often bring out—not only the best in us but the very worst as well, all our inadequacies and shortcomings, the things we would rather not see in ourselves, the tendencies we would rather not admit to possessing.

Instead of owning my limitations, I fell into the traps of blaming and fixing: blaming not only myself but those nearest and dearest to me for my "failures"; trying to fix and change myself and everyone around me in order to recapture the original unconditional love and acceptance I thought I could "get" out of my relationships.

One of the most difficult areas of growth for me was to recognize that the inherent beauty, the inherent *perfection*, in the design of all humans and human relationships is that they are "imperfect." We each have our weaknesses, our limitations, our blind spots. We each have our crabby days, our "down" days, our days of needing to be self-absorbed rather than giving. Yet somehow my expectations for myself were that I should always be there for those who loved me, whenever they needed me—and they for me. And that I should somehow be able to get on top of my "imperfections."

> *One comes in the end to realize that there is no permanent pure-relationship and there should not be. It is not even something to be desired. The pure relationship is limited, in space and in time. In its essence it implies exclusion . . . It excludes growth.*

When my efforts to make everyone and everything perfect continued to fail, I began to suspect that my basic assumptions about relationships were wrong, that no human being can ever meet another person's needs for unconditional love and acceptance one hundred percent of the time, no matter how much love is involved. I began to see that the only way out of the trap I had set for myself, the vicious cycle of failure and blame I had created with my unrealistic expectations, was to begin offering *myself* unconditional love and acceptance, and to forgive myself when I forgot to.

Ironically, my tendency toward perfectionism was the entry into my acceptance of imperfection. I had been hired to teach parenting courses at the local college. Determined to prepare "perfect" lectures, packed with all the right answers, I read voraciously on the subject of child development. After months of sorting and studying, I came up from under my pile of books with new eyes. Suddenly it was painfully clear to me that I had been going about this backward.

I loved my children completely and intensely—for who they were, not what they did. I loved them when they were tired and crabby, angry and sad. I loved them when they made mistakes. I wanted them to know they could count on my love and acceptance no matter how they were feeling or behaving. Why, then, didn't I love myself in the same way? Why couldn't I accept my own human frailties? Why didn't I give others the chance to love me for being *me*, not for what I did or how well I did it?

Wouldn't loving myself with all of my shortcomings, forgiving myself for my mistakes, laughing now and then at my imperfections instead of punishing myself, be the best role model I could provide for my children? Wouldn't this be the way I could teach them what I wanted them to learn most—that they were worthy and deserving of love all of the time, no matter what?

I realized it was about time I "fall in love" with myself—perhaps for the first time. I needed a few double-sunrise moments with myself.

> *The one-and-only moments are justified.*
> *The return to them, even if temporarily, is*
> *valid . . . these one-and-only moments are*
> *both refreshing and rewarding.*

My times of solitude began to take on another dimension. They became my "one-and-only moments." Moments when I prioritized myself, when I listened to *my* feelings and needs and wants. Moments when I stopped all the racing around I did for everyone else long enough to remind myself I was a good and worthy person deserving of my own love, acceptance, and appreciation. How could I expect others to love me if I couldn't love myself? And if I couldn't love myself, how could I love my children? If I couldn't accept my "imperfections," how could I accept my husband's? If I couldn't forgive myself, how could I forgive others?

I had to make a "leap," a leap of faith, over the gap of imperfection I perceived in myself, my relationships, and my life, to trust that love could never truly be shattered or destroyed. Only my limited concept of it had to crumble. (Thank goodness!) I had to come to a new understanding that love is not an end product chiseled out of the fulfillment of unrealistic expectations of a life—or a relationship—free of conflict. Love is constant. Love is steady despite my emotional ups and downs, despite my failures and disappointments, achievements and losses. Perhaps, most importantly, I had to recognize that sadness, anger, disappointment, and pain are not antithetical to love, but are, instead, signs of love. Signs of love growing, deepening; being refined like ore in fire.

Once I began to "be there" for myself—as the only one who fully knew and understood my deepest fears, my greatest hopes—then it only made sense that a commitment of equal strength was necessary in my relationship to others. In order to ride the rough waters and survive the breakers of relationships, I needed to commit myself to loving and accepting my partner and children completely, without trying to fix or change them. Once more faith was required. I needed to believe that love would continue through the struggles and pain, conflict, and imperfection inherent in human relationships. To believe that love not only survives, but actually flourishes in the very midst of life's hurdles.

The commitment that is required to weather the storms of relationships is not a blind-faith commitment, as I once thought. It doesn't mean denying our own wants, needs, and feelings, sacrificing everything for others. In fact, it means quite the opposite. It means loving and respecting ourselves enough to own our feelings and accept our needs. It means taking responsibility for healing our emotional woundedness.

Commitment in relationship means extending to others the same unconditional love, respect, and acceptance we offer ourselves. It is a commitment to the process of uncovering, over and over again, the love hidden in conflict. It is a commitment to self-inquiry, honesty, and vulnerability; mutual trust, respect, and compassion.

Relationships will always present their struggles —it is one of the few things in life we can count on— and I believe that is part of God's perfect design for them. Not only do the limitations inherent in relationships motivate us to turn within for strength, but each time we face the struggles and conflicts that relationships breed, the bond of mutual trust and love in the relationship is strengthened. Loving each other with all of our shortcomings is what gives relationships the richness and tenderness of intimacy.

As wonderful as those first few months of falling in love with Scott were, they pale in comparison to the deep, committed love we have for one another now, the love born out of seeing each other and our relationship through the many challenges that life brings. After years of arguing over how to load the dishwasher or whose responsibility it is to turn the heat down at night, or even struggling with more serious matters such as how to discipline our children or how to manage our finances, I can either pull my hair out in frustration, or laugh, knowing how much I would miss Scott if he were not the one here to argue with me. The pure infatuation I felt as a college coed still erupts in my heart at times, but now it is only one aspect of the rich, multidimensional love that we share.

One learns to accept that no permanent return is possible to an old form of relationship; and, more deeply still, that there is no holding of a relationship to a single form. This is not tragedy but part of the ever-recurrent miracle of life and growth. All living relationships are in process of change, of expansion, and must perpetually be building themselves new forms.

I no longer feel quite so compelled to fix things. I'm learning to accept and appreciate the times in between the double-sunrise moments of my life. I have a new image to hold in my mind now, a new image to replace the old, unrealistic dream of a life of continuous perfect double-sunrises.

It is the image of the sea, gently rolling and rising above the breakers along the shore, silently washing over the sand, sweeping away all the broken shells that lie scattered there. Flecks of color and smooth sharp shapes churn in her waves, tumbling over, around, and beneath one another. All the broken pieces create a fascinating design, a mosaic of depth and splendor.

I know each piece will resurface again, reshaped and freshly painted by the loving brush of the artist, the sea. A perfect double-sunrise shell might even burst forth now and again, if only for instant, to remind me of love's constancy, lying there undisturbed beneath the turbulent waters on the surface of the sea.

Love, I am beginning to understand, is not a fragile and fleeting thing like the double-sunrise shell. Love is deep and vast and eternal, like the sea out of which double-sunrise shells—and the double-sunrise moments of our lives—emerge, surprising us, as unusual and precious gifts freely given always do. Double-sunrise moments are gifts to celebrate, not swiftly passing illusions meant for us to try to recreate.

The sunrise shell has the eternal validity of all beautiful and fleeting things.

The perfect double-sunrise shell was almost my nemesis, but in the end, it became my redemptress. The shell that symbolized my greatest hurdle—to accept "imperfections" as perfectly acceptable—taught me to see there is perfection, even beauty, in brokenness.

. . . going deeper . . .

🌀 Imagine a beautiful little child sleeping sweetly after a long day of play. Imagine stroking that child's innocent cheeks, caressing that tender babe's head, singing softly to ease her fears and discomforts. Imagine that this little child had a difficult day, was overtired at times, stubborn and demanding, even unruly. Imagine any anger, frustration, and disappointment you may have felt toward that child being washed away in this moment of tenderness together. Now imagine that the child is you. Let yourself feel nothing but sweet tenderness, compassion, and joy at the marvel of you! *You* when you are tired, *you* when you are crabby, *you* when you are demanding, *you* when you are angelic and at rest in your heart. Sit quietly with yourself for a few moments and, then, record your feelings in your journal.

🌀 Consider a relationship that is particularly difficult at this time. What "negative" quality do you see in the other person? How might that person be mirroring something back to you that needs your attention? Be honest. Ask for humility. Ask for guidance. For example, if you are feeling angry and resentful because you have worked so hard and your spouse appears unappreciative, consider

whether you have appreciated yourself enough.
Did you push yourself too hard? Were the expectations you set for yourself too high? Did you forget to stop and do something loving for yourself?
If what you see in the other person truly feels unre-
lated to you, consider how you might best respond
to the situation when it arises again. You may
need to set better boundaries, take better care of
yourself so your "buttons" aren't so easily pushed.
Remember to remain the witness of your interac-
tions. Write your insights in your journal. You
might want to try writing with a crayon, this time
using your nondominant hand. By using your
nondominant hand, you let your intuitive side
speak; your heart answers rather than your head.

Consider creating a space where you can enjoy
some "double-sunrise" moments with yourself.
The corner of a room would suffice. If you'd like,
set out a small table or box covered with a beautiful cloth or piece of fabric. Place something you
cherish there. Let this be the first thing your eyes
fall on when you come to be alone, together with
yourself, and the last when you leave. Consider
adding a candle. You may want to add articles of
beauty or items that are precious to you —jewelry,
a stone, a shell, fresh flowers. Recognize that you
are honoring your inner beauty when you come
here to spend time immersed in stillness.

Oyster Bed

*I do not believe that sheer suffering teaches.
If suffering alone taught, all the world
would be wise, since everyone suffers. To suffering must be added mourning, understanding, patience, love, openness, and the
willingness to remain vulnerable. All these
and other factors combined, if the circumstances are right, can teach and can lead to
rebirth.* *

---

* From *Hour of Gold, Hour of Lead: Diaries and Letters of Anne Morrow
Lindbergh 1929-1932.*

Oyster Bed

Here is one I picked up yesterday. Not rare;
there are many of them on the beach and yet
each one is individual. You never find two
alike. Each is fitted and formed by its own
life and struggle to survive. It is an oyster,
with small shells clinging to its humped
back . . .

It suggests the struggle of life itself.

I woke up in the morning and looked out the small
window in my tiny monastic room. Something inside
me knew it was right to come here, to St. Benedict's, to
be alone with myself as I struggled to complete the final
chapters of this book.

The view from my bedroom window was
breathtaking. It had snowed during the night, and the
towering grove of pines was frosted in the lightest blanket of white. Hills in the distance were a muted gray, set
against the soft blue, nearly white sky. And nestled be-

tween the distant hills and the towering pines was a mirror, a lake, brilliantly shining silver. I heard the heavy gears of the bells begin to churn, in preparation for their morning song.

I grabbed my jacket, vest, and sweater, slid on my boots, hat, and mittens, and headed out into the silent beauty of the winter morning. Each step I took broke through the quiet stillness with a soft, delicious crunching sound. The crystal white snow beneath my feet was decorated delicately with patterns of gold and brown lace made from dainty seeds dried by autumn's sun and scattered by winter's wind.

In my mind's eye I was a child again, falling back into piles of freshly fallen snow, gently embraced by the thick silence, lying completely still, not wanting the moment to end, staring up into the vast, eternal sky. I felt warmed by the glow in my heart despite the bitter, frigid air around me. I felt completely safe in a pure, silent, still world . . .

A wren called from her perch on the red-branched and berried bush beside me. "That's my favorite sound," I had told a friend just a few days before as we walked the abandoned tracks to the train trellis that crosses over the lake in our small town, "the song of a bird in winter, when everything is frozen and still."

"Did you know birds have two songs?" It was more of a statement than a question my friend Janet offered. "That song is its song of survival. It's very differ-

ent from the exuberant, joyful song of spring, when the
bird knows the world will be warm again." *Interesting*, I thought to myself, *that it's the song of
survival I love.*

When I was in graduate school, there were two
degree tracks a masters social work student could follow. One was the psychotherapy route, which required
courses and field work in the arena of family dynamics
and family counseling, and the other was in organiza-
tional administration. I picked the latter. "Psychotherapy is for psychology students," I used to protest
vehemently. It made me angry to think social workers
were wasting their time "navel-gazing" at their own and
other people's personal problems. There were other,
bigger battles to fight: poverty, social injustice, crime.

I protested a little too loud and a little too often.
The last thing I wanted to do was admit there
might be a few personal issues that I needed to look at.
Like my tendency toward perfectionism, my worka-
holism, my need to please everyone. Or my bouts with
depression. Or my inability to enjoy sex. Not only did I
not want to look, I didn't even want to *peek*. I'd rather
solve the problems of the inner city, the Third
World—anything—but problems of my own.

I came from a nice, solid, white-collar, church-
going family. Good students, moral people. But depression ran rampant in our family and extended family. In
reality, depression had been around for generations,

from what bits and pieces of family history I knew. That was the other thing that ran rampant: secrecy.

But, every family had a few ghosts in the closet, didn't they? I just wasn't interested in scaring any of them up. In grad school classes on family dynamics, when we were asked to come up with personal family scenarios to dissect, I literally squirmed in my seat. I heard all that stuff about dysfunctional families and the need to break the cycle of abuse. I heard about the important role therapy played in healing long-standing anxiety and depression. But I was sure none of it was relevant to me and my life.

Some years later, however, when I found myself at the end of my rope as a young mother, a voice in my head whispered, "Maybe you could see a counselor and get some help." I reluctantly thought I ought to listen. I picked up the phone and dialed the number for a counselor more than once, only to hang up when the phone started ringing. "I am not *that* depressed," I would convince myself. "I can get over this if I just try. After all, I have everything anyone could want—a great husband, beautiful children, my health. I must be crazy to be depressed—but not crazy enough to see a counselor." At least I hoped not. If I never called, I wouldn't have to find out for sure.

Actually, it wasn't for my own sake that I finally saw a therapist. It was for my children's sake. My oldest was only two when I started reading everything I could get my hands on about child development so I would be sure to raise her to feel better about herself and her body than I felt about me and mine. But I knew, deep down, I couldn't expect that to happen by reading the right formulas. I knew I was consciously and unconsciously giving messages to my daughter all the time. I knew I couldn't expect her to have a positive self-image if I didn't.

I finally faced the fact that I needed some help. On more days than I cared to admit, my children were living with an angry and depressed mom. Even I was growing tired of it. Too many nights I had gone to bed promising myself the next day I would be better—more loving, patient, and full of fun; hoping my kids were young enough to forget their mom with swollen eyes who cried so much of the time. But those "tomorrows" rarely came. I was running out of boot straps to pull myself up by.

For years I had defended my right to be crabby and angry. I worked so hard, I protested, that I had the right to lose my temper as often as I did. I also defended my inability to enjoy sex, despite the fact I was married to an incredibly romantic, tender, and patient man. How could I relax when I was so overworked? Who needs sex any how? It's just not that important. I was a good partner and mother despite my bouts with anger and sadness, and less-than-enthusiastic attitude toward sex. Let anyone prove the contrary. I did it all—cleaned house, cooked healthful meals, orchestrated all kinds of elaborate family celebrations and fun, while holding down a part-time job.

> *[The oyster] is untidy, spread out in all directions, heavily encrusted with accumulations and . . . firmly imbedded on its rock.*

As the thick crust of my shell, accumulated over years of trying to "do it all," was beginning to crack, I argued with myself: Did it matter that I collapsed into tears or fits of anger and resentment, late at night when the kids were tucked in bed? While they were awake, I attended to every need they had. When they said "jump," I asked, "how high?" I even started a school for them. There was no way my children were going to suffer, be hurt, be kept from being all they could be . . . even if I had to sacrifice my own life to make that happen.

Where did that script for motherhood come from? Where did that script for childhood come from? Where did that script for *life* come from? I never stopped to ask. I was set on automatic pilot.

Until I crashed.

And again grace rescued me, this time in the form of counseling.

Very slowly, I began to pry off the oyster shell that encased my heart.

Somewhere, somehow, in the very early years of my life I had been hurt, emotionally, perhaps sexually. My memories were vague and shrouded in mystery, but evidence—in my dreams, in my body, in my patterns of reactions to life—seemed to indicate I had absorbed the message I was not safe . . . I was not good enough . . . I deserved to be hurt . . . my needs didn't matter.

Like the oyster shell, each of us has been "fitted and formed by our struggle to survive." Our identities, as well as our outlook on life, are shaped by our childhood experiences and the messages we absorb from, or assign to, them. Some of us are shaped by alcoholism, death, divorce, chronic mental or physical challenges within our families. Others by poverty, racial discrimination, or neglect.

Like the oyster shell, each of us is unique but not rare. None of us knows a life without struggles, without hardships, disappointments, even devastation. None of us makes it to adulthood without experiencing some event or set of circumstances that breaks our heart, or chips away at our self-esteem and inner confidence. Like the oyster shell, we each have

fought to have that place on the rock to which it has fitted itself perfectly and to which it clings tenaciously.

The question is, will we use the jarring events of our lives as excuses or opportunities? As excuses to justify clinging more tightly to the rock, to further harden our shell so we are shielded from pain? Or as opportunities to break free of tired, old, useless patterns of being that no longer serve us?

I know I clung to my rock for a long time. In my mind, I had become such an ugly shell, I was too ashamed to tell anyone about all the feelings and thoughts I had locked up inside. I continually rationalized and justified them, or felt an enormous amount of guilt and shame because of them.

Thank goodness grace forced me to take my discontent seriously.

The signs that presage growth, so similar, it seems to me, to those in early adolescence: discontent, restlessness, doubt, despair, longing, are interpreted falsely as signs of decay. In youth one does not as often misinterpret the signs; one accepts them, quite rightly, as growing pains. One takes them seriously, listens to them, follows where they lead. One is afraid. Naturally. Who is not afraid of pure space—that breath-taking empty space of an open door? But despite fear, one goes through to the room beyond.

Grace led me through the door of my darkness into the room beyond as I began to pay attention to the signs I had mistaken for decay and followed them where they led . . . to counseling.

Once over the threshold, once I got past the fear of that first phone call and actually scheduled and showed up for an appointment, I found the support I needed to understand my anger and depression not as flaws in my character but as symptoms of woundedness. I began to understand that I was not an angry and depressed mother because I was a *bad* mother. I was angry and depressed because I was a mother who was hurt as a child.

Shame and fear are some of the thickest and hardest shells to break through. It isn't until we can come to accept that most of the things we are less-than-proud-of in our emotional and behavioral repertoire are the result of our attempts to survive hurt and pain—*not* inherent, irreversible flaws of character—that we can begin to have compassion for ourselves. It isn't until we can come to be fond of our particular oyster shell—the shape and expression our life has taken on in order to protect our vulnerable hearts and self-image—that we can be not only accepting of ourselves but of the circumstances that led us to this shell.

> *One tries to cure the signs of growth, to exorcise them, as if they were devils, when really they might be angels of annunciation.*

I began to see that the hurt I had endured as a child served me in some way. It was, after all, the over-protectiveness I felt toward my children, born out of my childhood fears, that led me to help create an innovative, alternative school. It was that same worry for my children's well-being that motivated me to research and study theories of child development which in time inspired me to write a book and teach classes on parenting and family dynamics.

However, being compassionate with myself did not preclude taking responsibility for making changes in my life and behavior. Clearly, the adaptations that had gotten me to this place in my life had outlived their usefulness. Being an overachiever and highly responsible may have paid off in school and on the job, but in my role as spouse and mother it was doing no one any good.

As I began to release the hurt and fear that had been trapped inside of me for so long, I began to see that I could grow—actually *benefit*—from the less-than-perfect circumstances of my life. This was not an easy process. It meant stripping myself of the barnacles and shells I had accumulated in order to feel safe in the world. It meant moving beyond the comfortable place on the rock to a place of trust. It meant shedding the shells I had accumulated to protect me.

Perhaps middle age is, or should be, a period of shedding shells . . . Perhaps one can shed at this stage in life as one sheds in beach-living; one's pride, one's false ambitions, one's mask, one's armor. Was that armor not put on to protect one from the competitive world? If one ceases to compete, does one need it? Perhaps, one can at last in middle age, if not earlier, be completely oneself. And what a liberation that would be!

I agree with Anne Morrow Lindbergh: In many ways, the oyster shell poignantly resembles the shape and expression of the middle years of life. But, by "middle years" I do not necessarily mean the years between the ages of forty and sixty. I think of the middle years of life as all those years when we are "in the middle"—in between a time of awakening and growing to maturation from that awakening. The middle years are all those years that come after one turning point in our life and before the next. Times when we shed old ways and embrace new. Most typically, the "middle years" occur when some event jars us, threatens our safe and comfortable position in life, the one we worked so hard to secure. And when that happens, as it inevitably will, again and again throughout our lifetime, we will be faced with a choice: Will we take that first step through the breathtaking, empty space of an open door?

And the time may come when—comfortable and adaptable as it is—one may outgrow even the oyster shell.

Gradually, I'm growing accustomed to life beyond the oyster bed. In the process of shedding my shells, I not only uncovered old wounds, but I uncovered a deep source of joy—the pearl—that lives in the heart of every child before she begins to close herself off in response to pain. I no longer view life's struggles as harbingers of defeat and despair. As I pry loose the shells, a new zest for life fills me, a new spontaneity and honesty that makes my relationships more integritous —if not at times more challenging. Now I am able to perceive difficult times as "angels of annunciation": gears churning before morning bells clang, the song of survival sung in the stillness before the joyful song-of-life returning can be released in all its splendor from deep within my heart.

. . . *going deeper* . . .

🌀 Think of the "shells" you have accumulated during your lifetime. What do they look like? What do they feel like? How do they serve you? Which shells have outgrown their usefulness? In your journal, draw or write about the images that come to mind as you consider these questions.

🌀 Set aside some time to reflect upon your past. If someone were to write or sing a song about your survival, what kind of song would it be? Use your journal to write about what you hear. What kind of sound is it? What kind of instruments? What kind of rhythm? What might some of the lyrics be? Is there a particular refrain that keeps coming back?

🌀 Has any event jarred you recently? Threatened your comfortable position in life? What do you find yourself "in the middle" of? Take some time to consider ways in which this might be an opportunity. Make some notes for yourself in your journal or tell a close friend what options occur to you.

Argonauta

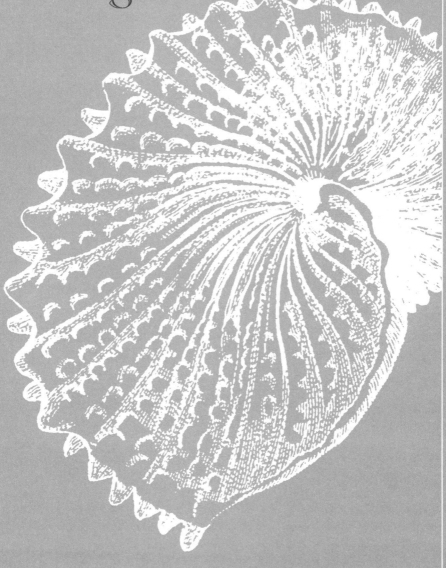

I felt a wonderful stream flowing through me that was this life—all this eternal life—going on, and it was joyful. *

---

* From *Locked Rooms and Open Doors: Diaries and Letters of Anne Morrow Lindbergh 1933-1935.*

Argonauta

There are in the beach-world certain rare creatures, the "Argonauta" (Paper Nautilus), who are not fastened to their shell at all. It is actually a cradle for the young, held in the arms of the mother argonaut who floats with it to the surface, where the eggs hatch and the young swim away. Then the mother argonaut leaves her shell and starts another life. I am fascinated by this image of the argonaut, whose temporary dwelling I have seen only as the treasure of a specialist's collection. Almost transparent, delicately fluted like a Greek column, this narcissus-white snail shell is feather light as some coracle of ancient times, ready to set sail across unknown seas.

. . . But what does the open sea hold for us?

When I decided to go to St. Benedict's to finish writing this book, I had every intention of sequestering myself away, focusing all my time, energy, and attention on the manuscript.

I have a confession to make: I'd been at the monastery for only two days when I snuck out . . . to the mall! To meet my kids and husband and do a little shopping. It was the last weekend before Christmas. I didn't even try to find a parking place in the football field—I mean parking lot—closest to the entrance. It was wall-to-wall cars outside and wall-to-wall people inside. And I loved every inch of it: every sight, every sound, every smell, every minute of being a part of the richness and diversity of human existence.

I felt like the mother argonaut, gracefully floating up from the deep, quiet waters of the past few days to the surface of life, teeming with hustle and bustle. We spent the afternoon *oohing* and *aahing* at possible gifts for Aunt CC and Uncle Wendell, Grandma, and each other, sipping Cokes and devouring French fries, standing in lines and then more lines, finally completing our purchases. Tired, but satisfied by our afternoon's adventure, we said our good-byes and I drifted back, alone, to the quiet depths of my still and silent room at the monastery.

The silence had thickened in my absence. All the weekend guests had gone home. No one even walked the halls softly outside the door of my room. I felt as though I'd slid beneath a warm, plush blanket. I curled up inside the quiet, closed my eyes, and looked back at the events of my day.

Up early this morning, I had decided to tidy my room. Quite a stack of dirty dishes had accumulated on my desk, next to my papers and computer. *Better wash them up,* I thought, *before I sit down to breakfast. Tomorrow I leave. No sense putting off all the cleanup until then.*

I walked down the hall to the kitchenette and filled the sink with hot, soapy water. It felt good to be engaged in the mundane task of washing and drying my own dishes. Comforting, relaxing. I became completely absorbed in the moment, in the luxurious warmth of the sudsy water, the delectable coolness emanating from the smooth ceramic tiles beneath my bare feet. Trance-like, I listened to the quiet hum of the refrigerator and the steady flow of rinse water. Glistening snow on the frosted window pane threw sparkling gems of sunlight across the room. Many moments must have passed before I noticed, out of the corner of my eye, that I was no longer alone. A woman, small of stature, stood next to me, silently preparing her own morning meal.

The quiet was so soft, so fragile between us —like a slumbering child—that I had no desire to disturb it. And yet I felt I ought in some way greet this woman who shared the intimacy of the golden morning's magic with me. Instead of giving voice to my greeting, I turned my head slightly and nodded. Just enough, I hoped, to express a silent welcome, yet not enough to stir either of us from our silk-spun reverie.

But as I turned my head, my eyes fell upon a beautiful brooch perched upon the woman's jacket. On it was a design—no, a symbol—that pricked something buried deep in my memory. Where had I seen that symbol before? I was intrigued. The pin called me back from my dream world, and I slipped through the sweet silence to ask the woman what the symbol meant.

A smile spread across her face as warm and tender as the stillness I had just disturbed. Quietly, the woman removed the pin from her jacket and began telling me its story.

She had received the pin while on a meditation retreat in the mountains of Colorado several years prior. The participants of the retreat had worn these pins when they wanted others to know they were observing silence. The symbol on her brooch, she explained, was a letter from the Hebrew alphabet. It was the letter *shin*, the first letter in the word *sheket*, which means "quiet."

"I wear it while I am here when I want the staff to know I am intentionally silent, contemplative, not sullen," she mused, "and if someone approaches me not knowing its meaning, I always try to remember to remove the pin first—before I speak— to uphold its intention."

Wouldn't it be wonderful, we agreed, if everyone had such a pin. Not only to wear while away from home and on retreat, but to be worn regularly while going about our daily lives. We laughed, thinking how many times it would come off and on again in the course of a mere hour, if worn by mothers of young children! We also confessed it might become habit forming—to slip the pin on whenever we felt tired and cranky, and wanted to be left alone (which might not be a bad idea, though not in keeping with the true purpose and spirit of the pin!). But then, quite seriously, we both speculated on the merits of having such a pin, if for no other reason, than to remind *ourselves* of the need to spend some part of each day quietly listening to the sound of our heart.

Holding the pin reverently in her hand, Judy introduced herself, and we continued our conversation, sharing bits and pieces of our lives over breakfast. The day's writing would have to wait.

As all good conversations do, ours meandered from one topic to the next, and then somehow landed on the subject of dancing. I mentioned to Judy that I recently attended a recital given by the school of dance my two oldest daughters attended. A number of young girls from our small town performed selections from "The Nutcracker" for a gathering of older women.

I found myself telling her how it had brought tears to my eyes to watch each young girl dance with a sense of her own grace and beauty. I was profoundly grateful they had an opportunity to experience their own magnificence, if only for an hour that day, leaping and bounding across the makeshift stage in the upstairs room of our stately, old library. I wished somehow we could all feel that confident and radiant as we danced through life.

It is, after all, like a dance, this life of ours. An ever-changing dance, requiring just the right balance of grace and effort if it is to be danced beautifully. Some of us rise to the surface to dance the dance of life single, some with a partner. Some dance the dance of mother, student, lawyer, teacher, corporate executive, volunteer, artist, healer. We might dance lavishly or timidly. Complex or simple steps. The combinations of style and form are unlimited.

But how does one learn this technique of the dance?

The lessons of the shells remind us. Each shell points us inward, to the beach of our hearts and The Sea of Inner Stillness, the source of love and inspiration. From that sacred space, the dance spirals out again, allowing us to bring what we find inside up to the surface —into our work, our relationships, the situations we encounter daily—the very things that, in this spiral dance, point us back inside once more, ever deeper.

At times, the dance of life is exuberant. We throw ourselves completely into our work, and it is invigorating. We want to spend every moment engaged in purposeful activity. We want to be right there on the surface of the water crashing on the rocks, having an impact on the world, dazzling in the sunlight. There is nothing quite like the exhilaration we feel when we allow ourselves full freedom to ride the crest of the waves as they come along. But, hopefully, we won't let the waves carry us so far away from the beach that we neglect the lessons learned there. No matter how exciting, how demanding our work may be, a certain level of creative energy can be sustained only if we take time to rest, time to play, time to eat well and exercise regularly. Time to return to *THE BEACH* to renew ourselves.

When our bodies are well-rested and nourished, alive and active, it is only natural to feel empowered to dance lively to the next tune that comes up. To have fresh enthusiasm, the willingness, and the desire to participate in life's dance to its fullest. And so we do. We join this committee or that committee, sign up for a course, start a project with the kids, begin playing with an idea for a new endeavor at work . . . and it feels wonderful. The stimulation of new challenges and new people is life-giving. We become caught up in the swirling movements of the jig. But then, little by little, the dance floor feels stifling, our feet tire. Our dance card is full, there is no time for a break. Gradually, the details of life accumulate . . . the check book needs balancing, the holiday decorations need to come down, this season's clothes need to be sorted through and packed away, next season's checked for size and surplus. But we have a class to teach or a class to take, calls to make and dates to break . . . enthusiasm wanes. To get back in step with ourselves, we need to remember to breathe. To slow down again. To remember the lesson of the *CHAN-NELLED WHELK:* simplify.

As we allow ourselves to breathe again, to slow down the pace at which we're whirling, we're able to see where changes in tempo and direction can be made. Changes that will keep the dance flowing, yet steady the beat to prevent things from spinning out of control—or coming to a grinding halt from sheer exhaustion. We might choose to step back from making further commitments in directions we are no longer headed. Or we might simply remind ourselves to not *over*-commit in directions we still want to go. We delegate responsibilities, postpone a project or two, let things rest, while we center ourselves, while we make time for solitude. Taking time for solitude allows us to listen carefully again to the sound of our inner music. We become aware of ways in which we can reset the pace of the dance according to our needs, our dreams, and our energy level. Predictably, the waning process reverses itself; zest for life begins to wax. Rejuvenated, we become full once more, like the *MOON SHELL.* Ready to dance again with others, ready to try new steps in the ever dynamic dance of life we find waiting for us.

Inevitably rejoining the dance going on around us leads to some tricky maneuvers. Dancing with kids, a partner, colleagues, and acquaintances gets complicated. We bump into each other at times, get tangled in each other's feet, step on each other's toes. Diversity inherent in the dance and dancers-of-life requires flexibility and openness to new and creative ways to adjust to the beat of others, while at the same time maintaining the integrity of our own unique style and flare. The beauty of the dance we compose with others reflects the beauty we find inside. When relationships become difficult, awkward, and clumsy, the *DOUBLE-SUNRISE SHELL* reminds us to dive back inside, into the deep and still waters of ourselves, to lovingly look at our own limits and imperfections so that we can see the inherent beauty in brokenness.

Then there comes a time when the music changes. Something in our lives changes, some event jars us, threatens our position in life, and becomes a catalyst for the "middle years." We become aware that we are weighted down with layer upon layer of fear, shame, and doubts that keep us from dancing the dance-of-life lightly, with love, spontaneity, and vulnerability. We're faced with shedding the shells we've accumulated to protect us, with moving off the rock we've become attached to. The *OYSTER SHELL* reminds us of the need to pry ourselves loose, to shed the barnacles and shells, to leave the familiarity and safety of comfort for the spontaneity and challenge of growth.

As we begin to move away from the clinging oyster bed existence we have grown accustomed to, we move closer toward the life of the *ARGONAUTA*, the life of moving gracefully between the surface of life and the deep still waters within.

In speaking of the argonauta one might as well admit one has left the usual shell collections. A double-sunrise shell, an oyster bed —these are common knowledge to most of us. We recognize them; we know about them; they are part of our daily life and the lives of others around us. But with this rare and delicate vessel, we have left the well-tracked beaches of proven facts and experiences. We are adventuring in the chartless seas of imagination.

Some of us dive daily into the uncharted waters within, others weekly, others yearly—in the prayers of our chosen spiritual tradition, in meditation, in quiet walks along the shore, in still moments stolen from our hectic day, in our office, in a skyscraper deep the heart of the city. We recognize we are not merely our shells—we are not our bodies, our thoughts, our emotions; we are not the work that we do, nor the roles that we play. We acknowledge that we are part of a larger stream of life that flows through all these things. When we accept this, we are free like the argonauta to float with, not fight against, the currents of life. Like the mother argonaut we are not fastened to our shells. From her, we learn to leave our shells for the abundance of the open seas. From the mother argonauta, we learn the rhythm of the dance,

> *a pattern of freedom . . . a natural balance*
> *of physical, intellectual and social life . . .*
> *the joy of living in the moment . . . One*
> *cannot dance well unless one is completely in*
> *time with the music . . . poised directly on*
> *the present step as it comes.*

As I turn the image of the argonauta over again in my mind, my thoughts take me back to the start of this day, where all this talk of dancing began, between Judy and I.

I linger over the moment we said our good-byes. I recall that as Judy began to head for the door, she hesitated for a fraction of a second, and then turned to look back at me, to share with me one last thought.

"*Shin*," Judy began, "is also the first letter in the Hebrew word *Shalom*, which as you probably know, means peace. *Shin*," she proceeded carefully, as if unveiling a precious heart-held secret, "is also the first letter in another beautiful Hebrew word, *Shechinah,* which refers to the feminine aspect of God. I just thought you might find that interesting."

With that, Judy left.

I sat alone in the undisturbed quiet of the kitchenette, grateful for a morning spent in the company of such a kind and generous woman. Her pin had brought me up to the surface of life, and now its meaning drew me back inside.

I was absorbed in the still waters again. Quiet . . . peace . . . the feminine aspect of God.

I left the warm embrace of the sunny room where we had talked and eaten our breakfast together. Slowly I walked down the long hall that led to the phone at the other end. I called my husband and children. I began the dance again, the spiral dance from the depths to the surface. We made plans to meet later that day—at the mall, of all places.

The rhythm of the dance continues.

Sheket, Shalom, Shechinah.

How can one learn to live through the ebb-tides of one's existence? How can one learn to take the trough of the wave?. . . Perhaps this is the most important thing for me to take back from beach living: simply the memory that each cycle of the tide is valid; each cycle of the wave is valid; each cycle of a relationship is valid. And my shells? I can sweep them all into my pocket. They are only there to remind me that the sea recedes and returns eternally.

... *going deeper* ...

⊚ Think of the patterns and pace in your dance of life. In your journal, draw any images that come to mind that represent the pattern of your dance. Can you see any cycles that keep repeating? Journal about any changes you would like to make in the pattern you are currently in.

⊚ For the next week, give yourself permission to experiment with different rhythms of solitude and activity. Change the *amount* of time you spend in each mode. Change *when* you spend time in each mode. Change *where* you go for each mode. Change some aspect of *what you do* in each mode. Keep notes in your journal of what feels renewing and satisfying for you. Journal about ways you might incorporate some of these changes in rhythm in your daily life.

⊚ Consider a place where you can get away, to be alone for a few days. Perhaps there is a retreat center near you. Consider asking a friend if you can house sit while they are out of town. Or begin setting aside some money each month to put toward a weekend away. In your journal, make a commitment to yourself to take some time to get away alone to reflect on your life, your dreams, your goals, to spend time absorbed in your inner stillness.

A
Few Shells

Living is a more important art than any other one. *

* From *The Flower and the Nettle: Diaries and Letters of Anne Morrow Lindbergh 1936-1939.*

A Few Shells

I am packing to leave my island. What have I for my efforts, for my ruminations on the beach? What answers or solutions have I found for my life? I have a few shells in my pocket, a few clues, only a few.

Weeks have passed since I was at the monastery. I am home on a cold January day, not unlike that January day, two years ago, when I began my journey back to the sea. The day I retrieved *Gift from the Sea* from my shelves and set out to rediscover the lessons of Anne Morrow Lindbergh's shells.

Only today, the cat isn't curled up next to my Springer spaniel who is, as always, sprawled across the kitchen floor. Today she is snuggled in the crook of my arm, nuzzling my breast for warmth and comfort, purring with deep satisfaction. And today, I, too, am in a new and different place, a place more deeply satisfying.

My return to the sea didn't take me to an island. It didn't lead me to a remote inlet lined with long stretches of white sandy beach where I could lie in the sun or play in the surf, write undisturbed, or take long, leisurely walks gathering shells left by the tide.

My return to the sea took me to an island inside. To a quiet place where time and space stretched out before me, inviting me to retrace the footprints I'd left on the beach of my life. My return to the sea led me to the still shore of my heart where I could rediscover the wisdom of the "shells." And, at the end of this journey, I, like Anne Morrow Lindbergh, find myself musing, *What have I for my efforts, for my return to the sea?* I have a few treasures to hold close to my heart, a few reminders of all I learned on my journey back to the sea:

My everyday life. Who would have thought a beat-up old station wagon crammed with kids could be a vehicle for spiritual awakening? Or a cluttered house and a dirty drain? Or a question posed by a nine-year-old soaking in a tub?

It is easy to overlook the beauty and wisdom inherent in the common and everyday shells of our lives —our responsibilities at home, at work, in our community. Yet it is our daily responsibilities that can serve as our "reminder shells"—if we allow them to point us back inside to the beach of our hearts, where we can find the rest and rejuvenation we need to meet life's demands and opportunities with patience, enthusiasm, and creativity.

My committed relationships. Falling in love with my partner and my children was easy. Melting into the adoring eyes of someone I loved, being won over by the purity and innocence of my newborn babies, took no effort at all. But *staying* in love, or at least remaining committed to returning to love when love feels far away, is the real challenge.

Meeting that challenge is well worth the effort. Learning to view the struggles inherent in our most significant relationships as potential pathways to intimacy is a gift beyond measure. When we can see the "imperfections" in ourselves and those we are closest to through the eyes of vulnerability and compassion, we can see them as "diamonds in the rough," buried treasures, waiting to expand our capacity to love and be loved. When we take personal responsibility for uncovering the love buried beneath conflict, we open ourselves more and more to the process of giving and receiving the true gifts of love.

My friendships. Had it not been for my friend Elizabeth giving Anna *Gift from the Sea*, and Anna asking me if I had read it, would I, on my own, have found cause to rummage through my old books and begin this journey back to the sea?

Is the journey within, to The Sea of Inner Stillness, even possible without the love and support, the guidance of friends? The journey within is not easy. There may be dark and painful places we have to traverse in order to find the pearl inside. No one can go there for us, but having the reassurance of friends who have traveled the path as well, friends who will love and accept us when we fall and stumble, makes the journey richer, if not possible.

Good friends are a gift. Their presence reminds us to take time for good conversation and good fun, to slow down. They help us celebrate the simple joys in life —watching our children grow, watching our relationships with significant others mature, watching our work blossom, watching ourselves grow beyond the safety of the oyster bed.

My body. You would think it impossible to forget the shell of the body, impossible to ignore it as a storehouse and counsel of wisdom. It is our constant companion. Yet my return to the sea had to start with paying attention to my body—to its basic need for rest.

Our bodies are with us every moment of every day. Even while we sleep, our bodies remain vigilant, performing their duties so we can rest our mind and spirit, drift off to the world of dreams.

Our bodies know so much. They know our particular past. Our joys as well as our hurts and sorrows. They register all our memories, painful and pleasurable. Miraculously, our bodies even know to heal themselves. They know what they need, and they know when they need help.

Our bodies also hold the wisdom of generations past. The blood coursing through our veins, the cells of our skin, muscle, and bone are configurations of ancient water. Water that has been on this planet since the beginning of time, witness and sustainer to an unfathomable number of varied and diverse life forms.

These bodies of ours are tough shells that will endure much to protect us, to carry us through this life. But they are fragile shells nonetheless, deserving of our loving care and our deepest respect. When we take time to listen to our bodies, and the breath of life flowing through them, we will naturally find ourselves living more in harmony with our core, our inner essence.

My mind. I needed to step back from my mind to recognize it as a shell. So entangled had I become in its starfish-like appendages, reaching in all directions, I thought it was something that controlled me. Something that had me in its grip and would never let me go.

By learning to "witness" our thoughts, as one

would observe any fascinating specimen of life found along the sea, we can choose what we want our minds to focus on, what we want them to grasp and hold onto and believe in. We can live as starfish outstretched and open to the sun, or closed and hiding beneath the rocks.

When our minds are open, they are powerful instruments for reaching and grasping new dreams, new ideas. It is our responsibility to nurture the state of our minds, to provide ourselves with physical rest and healthful food, along with spiritual quiet and divine food for thought, so we remain open to God's light and love in the world.

My self. By resting my body and clearing my mind, I discovered a quieter core self, an inner peaceful essence that resides deep within the space of my heart.

This essence is subtle, subtler than our thoughts and our emotions, subtler than our actions or our physical sensations. Yet it is our life force, it is that which connects us to the Divine. Taking time each day to be with my essence, to let it wash over me, reminding me of the love and beauty inherent within my self and all life, is perhaps the most precious gift of all I discovered on my return to the sea. A gift not merely *from* the sea, but a gift *of* the sea—The Sea of Inner Stillness.

Our lives are so full, we are pulled in so many directions, it is easy to be distracted from the Source of our joy, our contentment. Thank goodness the Sea continually beckons us to return, to discover anew the gifts She has to offer and to offer in return our humble gratitude.

Each of us has a collection of "gifts from the sea," beautiful shells, unique treasures, teachers of wisdom. To discover them, to learn from them, to fully appreciate them, we need not travel to distant islands far from home. We need only discover our "island eyes":

> *For it is only framed in space that beauty blooms. Only in space are events and objects and people unique and significant—and therefore beautiful. A tree has significance if one sees it against the empty face of sky. A note in music gains significance from the silences on either side. A candle flowers in the space of night. Even small and casual things take on significance if they are washed in space, like a few autumn grasses in one corner of an Oriental painting, the rest of the page is bare.*

> *I must remember to see with island eyes. The shells will remind me; they must be my island eyes.*

. . . *going deeper* . . .

☙ Take time to consider what "gifts from the sea" you have collected in your life. What have the "shells" of your life taught you or given you? In your journal, choose some words or images to symbolize what you treasure most.

☙ How might you want to be reminded of these gifts on a daily basis? Is there some ritual, some symbolic gesture or image you want to create in your life to keep your "shells" near, in the forefront of your mind, close to your heart? If you have a space you go to be in solitude each day, consider adding something to symbolize your return to the sea.

☙ Consider making it a practice to begin or end each day by remembering something, or someone, some "gift" of life you are grateful for. You might want to create a beautifully scribed list of these gifts to review at times when you feel your life is "lacking" in some way.

The Beach
at My Back

*I*t is true, I think, that understanding is
the only thing that frees one.*

* From *War Within and Without: Diaries and Letters of Anne Morrow
Lindbergh 1939-1944.*

The Beach at My Back

I pick up my sisal bag. The sand slips softly under my feet, the time for reflection is almost over.

I understand, now, the feeling I had when I first laid eyes on my friend Anna's copy of *Gift from the Sea*. The feeling of being a lost child. A found-lost child. A child trying to steady herself, too big to collapse into a puddle of tears and rush into her mother's arms.

That feeling was a premonition, a knowing. A knowing that my return to the sea, my journey back through the pages of Anne Morrow Lindbergh's book, would eventually lead me home, home to myself. It was a knowing that, as much as I found comfort and inspiration in the beautiful words of *Gift from the Sea*, I could not hide in the shelter of their embrace forever. In order for Anne Morrow Lindbergh's treasures to be more than lofty ideas tucked away in the recesses of a young girl's mind, or in a yellowed paperback book gathering dust on a shelf, I would have to make them my own. I would have to travel within myself, alone, to my own Sea of Inner Stillness, to find its gift: the shells of my own life, the treasures that held truth and meaning for me. I would have to go back and find all the parts of myself that had become lost and forgotten. Left behind because I was either too frightened or simply unable at the time to embrace them with compassion. I would have to go back into my past and gather into my heart the hurt child, the starry-eyed adolescent, the harried young wife and mother, and thank them for all they taught me. I needed to be reunited with my own self. I needed to offer myself comfort and understanding— the shelter of my own heart, rediscovered on my return visit to the sea.

And perhaps, too, that feeling of unsteadiness I felt when I first set eyes on *Gift from the Sea* after so many years of separation was also another kind of knowing. A knowing that, in the end, there would be no pat answers to the difficult questions of life, there would be no formula for perfect happiness. There would be no "mother's arms" that could keep me forever safe and protected from the inevitabilities of life.

Life will continue to present its difficulties and hardships, losses and sorrows. The gift of the sea is not a magic cure-all, the fountain of youth, or a source for trouble-free relationships and existence.

For me, the gift of the sea is simply the understanding that there is a divine love residing within my own heart. A love that will remain constant through the pain and struggle of human existence.

Patience—Faith—Openness, is what the sea has to teach. Simplicity—Solitude— Intermittency . . .

My return to the sea has brought subtle shifts in my life. I began to take better care of myself, to heal old emotional and spiritual scars. I began to slow the pace of my daily existence some. I enjoy simple pleasures more consciously, I nurture my most precious relationships, including the relationship I have with myself. But in truth, much of my external life remains the same. My husband and I still fight over some of the same old things, my kids still have crabby days, and I lose my temper and crab back. The house still gets cluttered and I get irritated. I slip into the habit of over-committing myself and burn out. There are days I question the purpose of my life and the meaning of life in general. There are times when the beach feels not just "at my back" but a million miles away, unreachable.

One thing in my life *has* changed dramatically, however: I know when I need to return to the sea. When I have my bad days, I know I need to slow down, to breathe. When serenity feels far, far away, I know I need to return to the lessons of the shells: take care of yourself, be with yourself, quiet your mind. When I feel lost, hopeless and full of doubt, I know I need to return to the beach of my heart.

—for I believe the heart is infinite—.

It is in the quiet space of the heart that we discover and share the divine love dwelling within. It is in The Sea of Inner Stillness that our source for strength, for acceptance, for love lies. It is in the spiral dance to the deep waters of quiet and back to the surface of activity that we experience the joy and rhythm of life.

> *When we start at the center of ourselves, we discover something worthwhile extending toward the periphery of the circle. We find again some of the joy in the now, some of the peace in the here, some of the love in me and thee which go to make up the kingdom of heaven on earth.*

The time for reflection is never over. Life will always be a mystery, full of unresolved questions. *Gift from the Sea* led us to the shore, now it is up to each one of us to accept the invitation to return the sea. Because, as Anne Morrow Lindbergh graciously reminded us,

> *There are other beaches to explore. There are more shells to find. This is only a beginning.*

About Anne Morrow Lindbergh

For more information about the life, writings, and ongoing philanthropic work of Anne Morrow Lindbergh, readers may contact:

The Charles A. and Anne Morrow
LINDBERGH FOUNDATION
708 South 3rd St., Suite 110
Minneapolis, MN 55415-1141

(612) 338-1703
e-mail: lindfdtn.@mtg.org
www.mtn.org/lindfdtn/

The Lindbergh Foundation is a not-for-profit organization created to honor the lives of the Lindberghs and to further their shared vision of a balance between technological advancement and environmental preservation.

About the Author

*A*nne M. Johnson is a licensed clinical social worker with a masters degree in social work from the University of Minnesota, Minneapolis. She has counseled individuals and families in private practice and as a consulting therapist for a Madison-based employee assistance program, and she has taught courses in parenting and family dynamics. A frequent public speaker, Anne has been interviewed on Wisconsin Public Radio and Milwaukee television. The *Chicago Tribune* has featured her co-authored book, *The Essence of Parenting* (Crossroad/Herder, 1995). Since 1990, Anne has studied meditation and made it a practical part of her life. Anne lives in Lake Mills, Wisconsin, with her husband and three daughters.